Central Market

H·E·B

COOKS

DEDICATION

To our customers, our vendors, our Partners,
and, most of all, to John Campbell
for living by his motto, "It's about FOOD."

Central Market
H·E·B ^{SM}

COOKS

Central Market H·E·B
COOKS

This book is a collection of recipes and memories from
customers, Partners, friends and foodies in celebration of the first ten years of Central Market,
an extraordinary place for food.

Published by
H. E. Butt Grocery Company

ISBN: 0-9754376-0-7
Library of Congress Number: 2004107484

Thanks to the entire Central Market team and special thanks to the staff and students
at the Texas Culinary Academy.

Manufactured in the United States of America
by: Favorite Recipes® Press
an imprint of FRP
Art Director: Steve Newman
Managing Editor: Mary Cummings
Project Editor: Jane Hinshaw
Photographer: Mike Rutherford
Food Stylist: Mary Anne Fowlkes

First Printing 2004
25,000 copies

CHARLES C. BUTT
CHAIRMAN OF THE BOARD
CHIEF EXECUTIVE OFFICER

H.E.BUTT GROCERY COMPANY
646 S. MAIN
P.O. BOX 839999
SAN ANTONIO, TEXAS 78283-3999
(210) 938-8203

Over lunch back in the 1980s, several leadership people at H-E-B were musing over what might be created to lead the nation with a very special store—incorporating the quality of a Manhattan delicatessen, the freshness of a farmer's market, and the selection of a Parisian shop.

It was clear that customers' interests were changing rapidly and that a new approach was needed to meet evolving tastes.

Importantly, we realized that we had many people within H-E-B who were anxious to demonstrate their depth of experience and worldwide contacts in acquiring and displaying fresh foods at the pinnacle of freshness, flavor and quality. Giving these members of our staff an opportunity to show what they could do in a new setting was one of our principal motivations.

As a broad outline of the new concept came together, we asked John Campbell, a longtime H-E-B Partner, to lead this quest to create a new and different food shopping experience.

John proved to be a brilliant choice. He quickly assembled a diverse team of talented individuals who—working together—produced a magic store.

Within a few months, any time I asked John about something new in Europe or New York, I found that he had already discovered it or found something better. It's hard to get ahead of John on food topics.

Today, Central Market shoppers across Texas enjoy a distinctive food shopping experience—thanks to John and his dedicated team of talented leaders who together turned a dream into an exciting reality.

This first Central Market cookbook is dedicated to John, our Central Market team, and our suppliers around the world.

Finally, to our customers, who have been patient, supportive and encouraging during this journey, we send our **special thanks** for choosing to shop with us.

Charles

Serving Texans— 1905-2005

PREFACE

We had a lot of ideas about how to pack the full five-sense experience of Central Market into a book. We wanted somehow to convey the smell of fresh fruits and breads; the wild and surprising colors of extraordinary produce like blue mushrooms and maroon carrots; the exciting sensation of tasting an unfamiliar cheese; the happy buzz of shoppers as they steer their carts through the store to find a surprise around every corner.

We considered a pop-up book and a scratch-'n'-sniff book. We thought about a book of recipes from visiting celebrity chefs, a collection of dishes from our talented store chefs or a historical compendium of Texas regional dishes to evoke our company's long history.

We wanted our first cookbook to embrace the whole of Central Market— the cooking school, the amazing produce, the huge selection of wine and beer, the bakeries, the cheeses, the fishmongers, the butcher shop, the specialty and prepared foods inspired by cuisines around the world. But mostly, we want to share the excitement and the love of great food that make Central Market so unique.

In the end, we decided, as usual, to do it all. (Well, you may have to wait for the pop-up and scratch-'n'-sniff.) In this book, you'll find recipes, tips and great Foodie ideas from all parts of Central Market. But the best part is the memories, recipes, stories and anecdotes contributed by the most important people at Central Market. That's you.

CONTENTS

FIRST COURSES

Appetizers
Salads
Soups

At Central Market, we only have one rule about the first course:

Always serve one.

No need to fret about French terms like "amuse-bouche" and "canapé."

It doesn't matter whether you pass the food, serve it at the table or

let everybody help themselves and dip. Food served before a meal

really only has one purpose—to get your taste buds excited

and give you a chance to get to know the other folks at the party.

In other words, the first course should introduce your guests

to both flavors and friends.

So our general idea of a great first course is any food that breaks the ice

and whets the appetite so that the meal—and the company—

that follows can be fully savored.

But the truth is, the first course is often the most exciting

part of the meal, because it gives the cook a great opportunity to

think outside the box (or the plate), to try something new,

exciting, exotic—even, sometimes, weird.

Go for it.

CM carries Crottin de Champcol, probably the most famous cheese of the Loire Valley. It is a goat cheese produced since the 16th century in the village of Champcol.

What is it about melted cheese? Few foods combine comfort and sophistication so handily. Think grilled cheese, onion soup, chile con queso and that old seventies favorite, fondue. Central Market Partners have suggested some other great ways to use melted cheese.

Remove the paper or labels from a wheel of Camembert and return the cheese to its wooden box. Poke holes all over the cheese with a wooden pick and sprinkle it with white wine. Replace the top of the box and place the whole thing in a 300-degree oven for 5 to 10 minutes. Serve it in the box with bread and charcuterie on which to smear it.

Brush pre-baked pastry shells with whole grain mustard. Top with a chunk of melting cheese, such as provolone, Brie, Swiss, even chèvre. Sprinkle with slivers of oil-packed oven-dried tomatoes and fresh thyme and bake at 350 degrees for 8 to 10 minutes.

Drizzle baguette slices with olive oil and toast until crisp. Blend equal parts of Gorgonzola cheese and unsalted butter, spread on each crouton and top each with a slice of fresh fig. Broil for 1 to 2 minutes.

Crottin de Champcol with Thyme and Honey

2 tablespoons fresh thyme leaves
1/4 cup honey
4 Crottins de Champcol cheese

rustic French bread, such as pain de campagne
sea salt and freshly ground pepper to taste

SERVES 12

Combine the thyme with the honey in a small saucepan. Heat over low heat to infuse the flavors.

Cut each Crottin horizontally into thirds. Cut the bread into rounds the size of the Crottin rounds. Place 1 slice of cheese on each slice of bread and arrange on a baking sheet. Bake at 350 degrees for 8 to 10 minutes or just until the cheese is softened and golden brown.

Drizzle the cheese with the thyme honey and sprinkle lightly with sea salt and pepper. Serve as an appetizer or with a salad tossed with a nonsweet vinaigrette.

Caponata

1 medium onion, chopped

1 rib celery, chopped

1 tablespoon extra-virgin olive oil

1 medium eggplant, peeled and cut into $1/2$-inch pieces

$1/3$ cup white wine

1 (14-ounce) can diced tomatoes

1 (6-ounce) can tomato paste

5 to 7 garlic cloves, chopped

1 tablespoon balsamic vinegar

1 teaspoon dried thyme

1 teaspoon dried basil

1 teaspoon dried oregano

$1/4$ cup chopped kalamata olives

1 tablespoon capers

salt and pepper to taste

SERVES 16

Sauté the onion and celery in the olive oil in a saucepan over medium heat until translucent. Add the eggplant and white wine and simmer for 15 minutes or until the eggplant and onion are tender.

Stir in the tomatoes, tomato paste, garlic, balsamic vinegar, thyme, basil and oregano. Simmer, covered, for 20 to 30 minutes or until the desired consistency. Remove from the heat and stir in the olives and capers.

Cool to room temperature and season with salt and pepper. Serve at room temperature with baguette slices or crackers.

You may prepare this up to 2 days in advance and store in the refrigerator.

Mediterranean Salsa

1 1/2 cups finely chopped
Roma tomatoes

1/2 cup finely chopped red onion

1/4 cup chopped kalamata olives

2 garlic cloves, crushed

3 tablespoons capers

1/4 cup balsamic vinegar

1/3 cup extra-virgin olive oil

1/4 cup finely chopped
fresh oregano

1 teaspoon kosher salt

1/4 teaspoon freshly
cracked pepper

1/2 cup roasted pine nuts

MAKES 2 1/2 CUPS

Combine the tomatoes, onion, olives, garlic and capers in a shallow bowl. Add the balsamic vinegar, olive oil, oregano, kosher salt and pepper and mix well.

Marinate at room temperature for 1 hour. Stir in the pine nuts. Serve with pita chips.

You may toss the salsa with cooked pasta and add 1/2 cup crumbled feta cheese to create a fabulous main dish.

Jane, a passionate cook who has traveled all over the world to eat, had the perfect qualifications to be one of our original Foodies. At Central Market, that's a capital "F" because this is the only place where "Foodie" is a job description.

We're all foodies here, of course, but some of us are Foodies— the people in green-striped aprons whose sole concern is customer service. If you don't know which of the hundred salsas will go best with your brisket, ask a Foodie. Besides knowing food, they know the whole store better than anyone. In fact, before you become a Foodie, you have to take a Foodie quiz with questions like: What's the best way to marinate sea bass? And what's a good substitute for angel food cake? And how do you put together a party for 20 in half an hour?

Good question.

Creamy Chipotle Dip

1 or 2 chipotle chiles in adobo sauce

2 or 3 garlic cloves

1/2 small onion

16 ounces cream cheese, softened

1 cup (8 ounces) sour cream

2 tablespoons adobo sauce

1 to 2 teaspoons ground cumin, or to taste

salt to taste

MAKES 3 1/2 CUPS

Combine the chiles, garlic and onion in a food processor and process until finely chopped.

Add the cream cheese, sour cream, adobo sauce, cumin and salt, processing to mix well after each addition. Serve with tortilla chips.

The debate about the best beverage to offset chile heat never ends in Texas. Some say milk, some say margaritas, some say don't drink anything—eat bread. Or butter. Central Market carries over 700 beers, but we stick by Mexican beer on this point, and there's a reason why. The heavy malt content of beers such as Mexican lagers provides a smooth, cooling sensation as it dissipates the heat from capsaicin. Beers that are high in hops are also a good bet. You'll want to avoid a watery beer because all that will do is spread the oily capsaicin around your mouth.

That seventies dish is back, but we are so much more cheese savvy than we were in the polyester decade. Just remember that the trick to fondue is to use more than one type of cheese. Be adventurous and change up your cheesy dip with these ideas from Central Market's cooking school. Follow the directions in the fondue recipe, using Brie, Roquefort and wild mushrooms; Cheddars, beer and mustard; Cheddars, curry and mango chutney; Monterey Jack and Pepper Jack with smoky salsa; or Fontina, Swiss and Parmesan with walnuts and basil pesto.

Fondue Suisse

1 garlic clove, cut into halves

1 tablespoon cornstarch

1 cup dry white wine

2 cups (8 ounces) cubed Swiss Emmental cheese

2 cups (8 ounces) cubed Gruyère cheese

freshly ground pepper to taste

3 tablespoons Kirsch

1 loaf French bread, cut into cubes

SERVES 4

Rub the cut garlic on the inside of an earthenware fondue pot or heavy saucepan; discard the garlic.

Blend the cornstarch with a small amount of the wine in a cup. Pour the remaining wine into the fondue pot and bring to a boil. Add the cheeses gradually, stirring until they are melted and blended.

Stir in the cornstarch mixture and pepper. Cook for 2 minutes or until the mixture is thickened and creamy; do not allow to boil. Stir in the Kirsch.

Keep warm in the fondue pot or spoon into a chafing dish. Place the bread cubes on 4 plates and provide long-handled forks for dipping.

Serve with a chilled dry white wine. You may also serve with fresh fruit.

CM always has genuine Swiss Emmental, a cheese with marble-size holes evenly distributed throughout, a melt-in-the-mouth texture and a distinctly nutty taste.

Curried Chutney Cheesecake

Cheesecake

1 cup lightly toasted chopped pecans

1/2 cup toasted flaked coconut

16 ounces cream cheese, softened

1/2 cup fruit chutney

2 eggs

1/2 cup thinly sliced green onions

1/2 teaspoon minced garlic

2 teaspoons curry powder

1/2 teaspoon salt

1/4 teaspoon cayenne pepper

Chutney Topping

1/2 cup fruit chutney

1/2 cup toasted chopped pecans

3/4 cup sliced green onions

SERVES 8 TO 12

For the cheesecake, butter the bottom and side of a 7-inch springform pan. Mix the pecans and coconut in a bowl. Sprinkle half the mixture over the bottom of the prepared pan.

Beat the cream cheese in a mixing bowl until fluffy. Beat in the chutney gradually. Add the eggs, green onions, garlic, curry powder, salt and cayenne pepper and mix well. Spoon into the prepared pan.

Bake at 300 degrees for 48 to 55 minutes or until firm. Cool to room temperature. Chill for 2 hours. Place on a serving plate and remove the side of the pan. Press the remaining pecan mixture over the side of the cheesecake.

For the topping, spread the chutney over the top of the cheesecake. Sprinkle some of the pecans around the edge of the cheesecake. Sprinkle some of the green onions in a circle inside the pecans, then the remaining pecans and the remaining green onions, forming 4 concentric circles.

You may also top the cheesecake with mango chutney or substitute macadamias for the pecans.

16

Pam's Pimiento Cheese

2 cups (8 ounces) shredded sharp yellow Cheddar cheese

2 cups (8 ounces) shredded mozzarella cheese

1 (4-ounce) jar diced pimientos

1/2 teaspoon sugar

1 teaspoon garlic powder

1 tablespoon minced fresh dill weed

1/4 to 1/3 cup mayonnaise

salt and freshly ground pepper to taste

MAKES 2 1/2 CUPS

Mix the Cheddar cheese and mozzarella cheese in a medium bowl. Add the undrained pimientos, sugar, garlic powder and dill weed.

Add enough mayonnaise to make the desired consistency and toss lightly to mix well. Season with salt and pepper.

The folks who work at Central Market tend to get very involved with their food. Many of our recipes and products were developed, not by chefs, but by Central Market staff, a group of in-house foodies who love to play around in the kitchen. Believing that good cooking knows no boundaries, they never hesitate to stray outside their own areas of expertise.

Our incredible Central Market tortillas? Our French cheese expert, Edouard, a former baker, came up with the recipes—one kind is made with butter, of course.

You'll see Manny in the morning at the Westgate store, steadily stirring the roux for his special gumbo.

And our basic pimiento cheese was elevated to a new, garlic-and-dill-flavored excellence by Pam, whose job at the time was stocking the Chef's Case at the first store.

Wild Mushroom Strudel

28 ounces mixed shiitake, oyster,
cremini, portobello and
button mushrooms

2 shallots, chopped

2 garlic cloves, minced

1 tablespoon chopped fresh basil

2 teaspoons chopped fresh thyme

3 tablespoons butter

1/4 cup pine nuts, toasted

salt and pepper to taste

8 sheets phyllo pastry

5 tablespoons butter, melted

1 teaspoon chopped fresh thyme

SERVES 6

Clean, trim and coarsely slice the mushrooms. Sauté the shallots, garlic, basil and 2 teaspoons thyme in 3 tablespoons butter in a skillet until the garlic is tender. Add the mushrooms and sauté for 15 minutes or until very tender. Stir in the pine nuts and season with salt and pepper.

Layer 2 sheets of phyllo on a kitchen towel on a flat surface; cover the remaining phyllo with plastic wrap and a damp towel. Brush the phyllo with some of the melted butter and top with 2 phyllo sheets. Brush with butter and sprinkle with half the remaining 1 teaspoon thyme. Layer with 2 phyllo sheets, brush with butter and sprinkle with the remaining thyme. Top with the remaining phyllo sheets and brush with butter.

Spoon the mushroom mixture in a line 2 inches from a long edge, leaving a 2-inch edge at the top and bottom. Fold the narrow edges over the filling and brush the folded edges with butter.

Roll the phyllo to enclose the filling, starting at the long edge closest to the filling and lifting the towel to help roll. Lift the roll with a spatula and place seam side down on a buttered baking sheet. Place in the freezer for 5 minutes.

Brush with butter. Bake at 350 degrees for 15 minutes or until golden brown. Cut into slices to serve.

This can also be served as a meatless main course for 4 persons.

Wild Mushroom and
Goat Cheese Quesadillas

8 ounces mixed shiitake, cremini and oyster mushrooms, sliced

1/4 cup julienned red bell pepper

1/4 cup julienned green bell pepper

2 tablespoons olive oil

1 teaspoon chopped garlic

2 tablespoons chopped green onions

7 ounces goat cheese, crumbled

8 Central Market Southwest flour tortillas

SERVES 8

Sauté the mushrooms and bell peppers in the olive oil in a skillet for 4 minutes. Add the garlic and green onions. Sauté for 2 minutes or until the vegetables are tender. Remove from the heat and stir in the goat cheese.

Spread the mushroom mixture over 4 of the tortillas. Top with the remaining tortillas. Grill on a flat griddle or in a large skillet until golden brown on both sides.

Cut each quesadilla into 6 wedges and arrange on a serving plate. Serve with Central Market Mango Salsa and guacamole.

CM Southwest flour tortillas get their color and flavor from chili powder and jalapeño chiles. Keep them on hand, make the filling for these quesadillas in advance and you can finish them any time your appetite kicks in.

Salmon-Stuffed New Potatoes

12 (1-inch) red potatoes

5 ounces smoked salmon, finely minced

2 tablespoons finely minced red onion

1 tablespoon finely minced chives

1 tablespoon lemon juice

1 teaspoon finely chopped lemon zest

1/4 cup sour cream or crème fraîche

salt and pepper to taste

crème fraîche and small dill sprigs

SERVES 6

Combine the potatoes with enough cold water to cover in a large saucepan. Bring to a boil over high heat. Reduce the heat and simmer for 10 to 15 minutes or just until tender; do not overcook. Drain and rinse with cold water to stop the cooking process. Cool to room temperature.

Combine the salmon, onion, chives, lemon juice, lemon zest and sour cream in a medium bowl. Season with salt and pepper and mix well. Cover and let stand while preparing the potatoes.

Cut each potato into halves lengthwise. Scoop out a small well in the cut side of each potato with a melon baller. Remove a thin slice from the rounded side of each potato so it will sit flat.

Spoon a small amount of the salmon mixture into each potato well. Arrange on a serving platter and top each with a small dollop of crème fraîche and a small sprig of dill. Serve at room temperature.

You may cook the potatoes up to 24 hours in advance and chill until time to fill.

For variety, the potato shells may be deep-fried, and steamed or fried slices may be used instead of the shells. Also, 1/2-inch slices of cucumber may be substituted for the potato shells and caviar may be substituted for the dill sprigs.

Clams with Pancetta and Red Pepper Coulis

Red Pepper Coulis

2 large roasted red bell peppers,
coarsely chopped

2 large garlic cloves

1 teaspoon grated lemon zest

1 tablespoon chopped
fresh marjoram

1 1/2 tablespoons olive oil

salt and pepper to taste

Clams

32 clams, cleaned

4 (1-ounce) slices pancetta, cut into 32 pieces

SERVES 6 TO 8

For the coulis, combine the bell peppers, garlic, lemon zest and marjoram with the olive oil in a food processor. Process until smooth. Season with salt and pepper.

For the clams, line a large baking pan with foil. Arrange the clams in the prepared pan. Bake at 500 degrees for 7 to 8 minutes or until the clams open, discarding any clams that do not open. Let stand until slightly cooled.

Remove and discard the top shells of the opened clams. Top each clam with 1 teaspoon of the coulis and 1 piece of pancetta. Broil for 3 to 5 minutes or until the pancetta browns. Arrange on a serving plate and garnish with lemon wedges.

Bacon is usually a cut of meat from the belly of the pig (that's right, pork bellies). Pancetta is Italian-style bacon, rolled, cured and not smoked like American bacon. Bacon—pancetta included—gets a bad rap for fat, but it is so flavorful that a small amount takes a dish from pedestrian to outrageous. The secret is to render it, or cook it slowly, so the fat is released. Render pancetta, sauté some peeled and deveined shrimp in the drippings, add some creamy Gorgonzola cheese, and you've got a pasta sauce to die for. Rendered pancetta tossed with balsamic vinegar over spinach and frisée makes a great salad. Top it with a grilled chicken breast, and you've got dinner.

Irish author Jonathan Swift famously said, "He was a bold man who first ate an oyster." Central Market's oysters are carefully monitored and refrigerated to ensure safety and freshness. They are available year-round, so you can pretty much forget that business about months with the letter "r," though it is true that you'll find the plumpest and most flavorful Gulf oysters during the fall and winter.

Texas Gulf Oysters have a special place in our hearts, and are great for cooking. Louisiana provides us with Gold Band Oysters, pressure-treated to remove bacteria; the pressure also loosens the oysters from the shells so they can be shucked easily. Swift summed it up: Oysters are discouragingly ugly, but courage has its rewards.

Oyster Cocktail

4 Roma tomatoes, chopped

1 bunch cilantro, chopped

1 white onion, chopped

2 serrano chiles, chopped

4 garlic cloves, minced

3 to 4 cups ketchup

1/4 cup olive oil

lime juice to taste

salt and pepper to taste

24 to 36 fresh oysters, cleaned

SERVES 4 TO 6

Combine the tomatoes, cilantro, onion, chiles and garlic in a bowl. Add the ketchup, olive oil and lime juice. Season with salt and pepper and mix well.

Add the oysters and stir to coat well. Spoon into cocktail glasses and serve with crackers.

Tequila Shrimp

2 tablespoons chopped seeded
jalapeño chile

1 tablespoon chopped garlic

1 tablespoon chopped fresh
cilantro

1^1/$_2$ tablespoons tequila

^{1}/$_3$ cup fresh lime juice

2 teaspoons olive oil

^{1}/$_2$ teaspoon coarse salt

^{1}/$_8$ teaspoon white pepper

2 pounds shrimp, cooked, peeled
and deveined

SERVES 8

Combine the chile, garlic and cilantro in a large bowl. Add the tequila, lime juice and olive oil. Season with salt and white pepper and mix well.

Add the shrimp and stir to coat well. Marinate, covered, in the refrigerator for 30 minutes to 1 hour. Drain and serve over ice.

Spring Mix with Toasted Pecans, Cranberries and Stilton in Sherry Vinaigrette

Orange Toasted Pecans

1 1/2 teaspoons grated
orange zest

1/2 cup sugar

2 tablespoons Central Market
freshly squeezed orange juice

2 cups pecan halves

Sherry Vinaigrette

1 tablespoon Dijon mustard

3/4 teaspoon sugar

3 tablespoons sherry
wine vinegar

6 tablespoons extra-virgin
olive oil

salt and pepper to taste

Salad

8 ounces organic
spring mix greens

1 cup dried cranberries

1 1/2 cups (6 ounces) crumbled
Stilton cheese

1 cup Orange Toasted Pecans

salt and pepper to taste

SERVES 6

For the pecans, combine the orange zest, sugar and orange juice in a large saucepan. Bring to a boil. Add the pecan halves and mix well. Cook for 3 to 5 minutes or until the pecans are well coated, stirring constantly with a slotted spoon and being careful not to burn the pecans. Spread on waxed paper to cool.

For the vinaigrette, combine the Dijon mustard, sugar and vinegar in a bowl and whisk until smooth. Add the olive oil gradually, whisking constantly until mixed. Season with salt and pepper.

For the salad, toss the greens with the vinaigrette in a bowl. Spoon onto serving plates and top with the cranberries and Stilton cheese. Sprinkle with 1 cup of the pecans and season with salt and pepper.

You may serve the unused pecans as a snack or freeze and reserve them for another use.

Field Greens with a Tangy Blood Orange and Pear Vinaigrette

Tangy Blood Orange and Pear Vinaigrette

3/4 tablespoon minced garlic

3/4 tablespoon chopped peeled gingerroot

1/2 bunch green onions, white portions only, chopped

1 ripe pear, peeled and chopped

1/4 cup olive oil

juice of 5 blood oranges, strained

1/2 habanero chile

1/2 cup rice wine vinegar

1/4 cup black sesame seeds

salt to taste

1/4 cup olive oil

Salad

12 ounces mixed field greens

1 yellow bell pepper, chopped

1 red bell pepper, chopped

16 ounces baby bok choy, sliced

blood orange slices

1 ripe pear, peeled and chopped

SERVES 8

For the vinaigrette, sauté the garlic, gingerroot, green onions and pear in 1/4 cup olive oil in a skillet until light brown. Add the orange juice and chile. Cook until the liquid is reduced by half. Remove the chile and strain the liquid into a mixing bowl. Whisk in the vinegar, sesame seeds and salt. Add 1/4 cup olive oil gradually, whisking until smooth.

For the salad, combine the field greens, bell peppers and bok choy in a salad bowl and toss to mix. Add the vinaigrette and toss to coat well. Spoon onto serving plates. Top with the orange slices and chopped pear.

Baby Spinach, Fig and Goat Cheese Salad with Apple Rosemary Vinaigrette

Apple Rosemary Vinaigrette

$1/3$ cup apple jelly

1 tablespoon roasted garlic purée

1 tablespoon chopped shallots

$1/2$ serrano chile

$1/2$ cup white balsamic vinegar

$1 1/2$ teaspoons fresh rosemary leaves

$3/4$ cup canola oil

$3/4$ cup extra-virgin olive oil

salt and pepper to taste

Salad

$1/4$ cup julienned Serrano ham

olive oil

4 cups fresh baby spinach

4 fresh figs, sliced

1 cup (4 ounces) crumbled Humboldt Fog goat cheese

SERVES 4

For the vinaigrette, combine the apple jelly, garlic purée, shallots, chile, balsamic vinegar and rosemary in a food processor or blender. Add the canola oil and olive oil gradually, processing constantly until smooth. Season with salt and pepper.

For the salad, fry the ham in a small amount of olive oil in a skillet over medium heat just until crisp; do not overcook. Remove with a slotted spoon to paper towels to drain.

Combine the ham with the baby spinach, figs and goat cheese in a salad bowl and mix well. Toss with enough of the vinaigrette to coat lightly. Spoon onto salad plates.

Store the unused portion of the vinaigrette in the refrigerator and reserve for another use.

CM Tuscan Tuna Salad

8 ounces yellowfin tuna

10 to 11 ounces albacore tuna

1/2 small red onion, minced

1/3 cup minced fennel bulb

2 teaspoons minced garlic

1/3 cup coarsely chopped
kalamata olives

2 tablespoons drained capers

2 tablespoons finely chopped
fresh basil

3 tablespoons finely chopped
fresh parsley

3 tablespoons mayonnaise

2 tablespoons olive oil

2 tablespoons balsamic vinegar

salt and pepper to taste

SERVES 4

Steam or poach the yellowfin tuna and albacore tuna for 12 to 15 minutes or until cooked through. Drain and cool the tuna and flake into small pieces.

Combine the tuna with the onion, fennel, garlic, olives, capers, basil and parsley in a bowl. Toss to mix well. Add the remaining ingredients. Chill until serving time.

Tuscan Tuna Salad, dreamed up by Luis, one of our seafood managers, makes a great lunch or summer supper. If there's any left over, you're in for the most luxurious tuna melt in the universe. For more sandwiches off the beaten track, we looked in the lunch boxes of some CM Partners. Okay, there was lots of peanut butter, but besides that, here's what we found:

Deli ham and sliced cheese rolled up in butter lettuce to dip in CM Chipotle Aïoli; a CM scone spread with peanut butter from Bulk Foods, topped with banana slices and drizzled with honey; CM Whole Wheat Bread toast around mayonnaise, thinly sliced cucumber, provolone cheese, sliced tomato, sprouts, pickled ginger and fresh mint; a pita pocket filled with Hummus, sprouts and grated carrots from the Salad Bar with a bit of CM Pico de Gallo from the Bulk Bar; a homemade muffuletta made on CM Italian White Bread with Italian Olive Salad and meats and cheese from the Deli.

Lobster Salad with Spicy Pecan Vinegar and Vanilla Dressing

Spicy Pecan Vinegar and Vanilla Dressing

2 egg yolks

1 teaspoon Dijon mustard

1/2 teaspoon sugar

1 tablespoon fresh lemon juice

2 tablespoons Cuisine Perel spicy pecan vinegar

1 cup vegetable oil

1 teaspoon Mexican vanilla extract

Salad

1 head Boston lettuce

6 baby lobster tails, cooked and cut into halves lengthwise

1 avocado, sliced

1 (8-ounce) can artichoke hearts, drained and cut into halves

2 green onions, sliced

3/4 cup thinly sliced celery

3/4 cup sliced fresh mushrooms

SERVES 6

For the dressing, combine the egg yolks, Dijon mustard, sugar, lemon juice and vinegar in a blender and process until smooth. Add a few drops of the oil, processing constantly until smooth. Add the remaining oil in a fine stream, processing constantly until smooth. Stir in the vanilla.

For the salad, line 6 salad plates with the Boston lettuce leaves. Arrange the lobster tails, avocado and artichoke hearts on the plates. Sprinkle with the green onions, celery and mushrooms. Drizzle with the dressing.

Cooking, like theater, is an ensemble art, a kind of sensory collaboration between the chef and the diner. Sometimes Central Market finds itself right in the middle of the act.

We recall the time a customer needed four live lobsters for a very special dinner and was told to keep them in their natural habitat— water—until time to cook them. Several hours later, we received a frantic call: the lobsters had expired, died, gone to meet their maker. After explaining that a lobster's natural habitat is cold salt water— not warm tap water—we rushed over with four lobsters, very much alive. Another cooking tale with a happy ending.

Tamarind-Glazed Grilled Quail
on Spring Greens

Tamarind Marinade and Quail

$1/2$ cup minced shallots

$1/2$ cup soy sauce

2 teaspoons minced garlic

1 tablespoon tamarind
concentrate

3 tablespoons honey

$1/4$ cup cider vinegar

$11/2$ teaspoons minced
gingerroot

$3/4$ cup water

4 whole semiboneless quail

Salad

2 tablespoons extra-virgin
olive oil

2 teaspoons balsamic vinegar

salt and pepper to taste

4 cups mixed spring greens

SERVES 4

For the marinade and quail, combine the shallots, soy sauce, garlic, tamarind concentrate, honey, vinegar, gingerroot and water in a small saucepan. Bring to a boil. Reduce the heat and simmer for 2 minutes. Cool to room temperature. Strain, reserving the liquid.

Rinse the quail and pat dry. Combine with the tamarind concentrate marinade in a shallow dish or resealable plastic bag and mix well. Marinate in the refrigerator for 4 to 12 hours, turning occasionally.

Drain the quail and place on an oiled grill over medium-hot coals. Grill for 4 minutes on each side or until well browned and cooked through.

For the salad, combine the olive oil, balsamic vinegar, salt and pepper in a bowl and mix well. Add the salad greens and toss to coat well. Spoon onto 4 salad plates and top each with a grilled quail.

You may substitute chicken for the quail in this recipe.

Spicy Thai Lobster Soup with Lemon Grass

1 stalk lemon grass
6 cups chicken broth
1 small garlic clove, crushed
1 teaspoon grated lime zest
2 tablespoons lime juice
2 teaspoons fish sauce
1/2 teaspoon salt

8 ounces lobster tail meat, chopped
8 ounces enoki mushrooms, trimmed
3 tablespoons sliced green onions
2 tablespoons chopped cilantro
1 or 2 red chiles, seeded and finely chopped
cilantro and lemon grass

SERVES 6

Crush the stalk of the lemon grass with the dull edge of a knife and cut into 6-inch pieces. Bring the chicken broth to a boil in a saucepan. Add the lemon grass, garlic, lime zest, lime juice, fish sauce and salt. Simmer for 5 minutes.

Remove the lemon grass and garlic clove with a slotted spoon. Add the lobster. Cook for 2 minutes or until the lobster is pink and opaque. Add the mushrooms, green onions, 2 tablespoons cilantro and chiles. Cook for 1 to 2 minutes longer or until heated through.

Ladle the soup into soup bowls and sprinkle with additional cilantro and lemon grass.

Cooking, like theater, is an ensemble art. It's a kind of sensory collaboration between the cook and the diner, even when they are the same person. But occasionally, we're reminded that cooking is also a collaboration—though an unwilling one—between the cook and the dinner. We recall the time a customer needed four live Maine lobsters for a very special dinner.

We told her she needed to keep them in their natural habitat—water—until it was time to cook them. Several hours later, we received a frantic phone call. The lobsters had expired, died, gone to meet their maker. After we had explained that a lobster's natural habitat is cold salt water, not warm tap water, we rushed over to her house with four lobsters, very much alive. Another cooking tale with a happy ending—for everyone but the lobsters.

CM Tortilla Soup

2 tablespoons olive oil

1 1/2 cups chopped onions

1/2 cup chopped yellow
bell pepper

1/2 cup chopped red bell pepper

1 poblano chile, seeded
and chopped

1 tablespoon minced garlic

3 tablespoons ground cumin

2 1/2 to 3 cups chopped
tomatoes, about
3 medium tomatoes

2 quarts strong chicken stock

1 poblano chile, seeded
and chopped

1 1/2 cups shredded
cooked chicken

salt and freshly ground pepper
to taste

1/4 cup chopped cilantro

1 cup (4 ounces) shredded
Cheddar cheese

1 cup (4 ounces) shredded
Monterey Jack cheese

4 corn tortillas, cut into halves,
cut crosswise into 1/4-inch strips
and crisp-fried

SERVES 6

Heat the olive oil in a large stockpot over medium-high heat. Add the onions and sauté until translucent. Add the bell peppers, 1 poblano chile and garlic and sauté for 2 or 3 minutes. Stir in the cumin and cook for 1 minute, stirring constantly.

Add the tomatoes and chicken stock. Bring to a boil and reduce the heat. Simmer for 5 minutes. Stir in 1 poblano chile and the chicken. Return to a boil and season with salt and pepper. Remove from the heat and stir in the cilantro.

Mix the Cheddar cheese and Monterey Jack cheese in a bowl. Ladle the soup into bowls and top with the mixed cheeses and tortilla strips.

MAIN COURSES

Meat
Poultry
Seafood
Meatless

Remember old-fashioned school lunch trays and TV dinners?
They were neatly compartmentalized so the main dish
(always meat) didn't touch the vegetables and the vegetables
were clearly separated from the starch. No touching allowed.
That's not how we eat anymore. At Central Market,
we love to mix it up, break the rules a little.
Meat or chicken is plopped down on a mixed salad;
broiled fish is nested in mashed potatoes. The main dish
may or may not be meat; if it is, we may side it with fruit
instead of potatoes. If we do serve potatoes, they might be blue.
Food is supposed to be fun, remember?
We cook for recreation as much as nutrition, and we eat to
nourish the body and soul together.

Pan-Seared Filet Mignon with Cherry Port Reduction

Cherry Port Reduction

2 tablespoons unsalted butter

2 large garlic cloves, minced

2 large shallots, minced

1 cup ruby port

$1^1/_4$ cups beef stock or
low-sodium beef broth

$^1/_2$ cup dried cherries

Filets

2 tablespoons unsalted butter

4 (6-ounce) $1^1/_2$-inch beef tenderloin filets

salt and freshly ground pepper to taste

SERVES 4

For the reduction, melt the butter in a saucepan over medium heat. Add the garlic and shallots and sauté for 1 minute. Stir in the wine, beef stock and cherries. Simmer over medium-high heat until the sauce is reduced to 1 cup.

For the filets, heat a large skillet over medium-high heat until hot and add the butter, swirling the skillet to coat evenly. Season the filets with salt and pepper and add to the skillet; do not crowd. Cook for 5 minutes on each side for medium-rare. Remove the filets to a platter and cover to keep warm.

Pour the reduction into the skillet, scraping to remove any browned bits from the bottom of the skillet. Simmer until the reduction coats the back of a spoon. Serve with the filets.

Everyone has his own favorite comfort foods—slow-cooked dishes like these ribs frequently top the list. But Central Market has given the term new meaning. A lady stopped one of our operations managers one day to say, "You know, whenever I'm depressed I come to Central Market. Even if I don't need any groceries! I just come and wander around and look at what's new. And it works. When I leave I feel better." Women used to get a new hat to cheer themselves up. At Central Market, they're more likely to get a new kind of tangerine.

Spicy Margarita Short Ribs

4 pounds beef chuck short ribs

1 cup bottled nonalcoholic margarita mix

2 cups medium-hot chunky salsa

2 tablespoons tequila

2 tablespoons soy sauce

2 teaspoons grated gingerroot

2 teaspoons finely chopped garlic

6 curly green lettuce leaves

1 (10-ounce) package Mexican rice, cooked

2 large limes, sliced crosswise

SERVES 6

Sear the short ribs in a Dutch oven for 7 minutes or until brown on all sides; drain well. Remove the ribs to a 9×12-inch baking dish sprayed with nonstick cooking spray.

Combine the margarita mix, salsa, tequila, soy sauce, gingerroot and garlic in a bowl and mix well. Pour over the ribs and cover tightly with foil.

Bake at 375 degrees for 1 1/2 to 2 hours or until the ribs are tender and the sauce is thickened, turning the ribs occasionally; remove the foil toward the end of the cooking time if necessary to thicken the sauce.

Line a serving plate with the lettuce leaves. Spoon the rice into the center of the plate and arrange the ribs around the rice. Spoon the sauce over the ribs and garnish with lime slices.

Veal Chops Stuffed with Fontina and Prosciutto

4 (8-ounce) veal rib chops

4 (1/4-ounce) slices prosciutto

4 (1/4-ounce) slices fontina cheese

8 fresh sage leaves

extra-virgin olive oil

sea salt and freshly cracked pepper to taste

1 lemon, cut into 4 wedges

SERVES 4

Cut a pocket in the eye of the rib opposite the bone in each veal chop. Fold 1 slice of prosciutto around 1 slice of cheese and 2 sage leaves and stuff into the pocket of 1 veal chop. Repeat to stuff the remaining chops.

Brush both sides of the chops with olive oil and sprinkle with sea salt and cracked pepper. Let stand at room temperature for 1 hour.

Grill the chops on a grill preheated to 400 degrees for 6 to 8 minutes on each side. Remove to a plate and cover loosely with foil. Let stand for 5 minutes. Serve each chop with a wedge of lemon.

Fanatical is a strong word, but many Central Marketers—Partners and customers—are proud of the label. When the first store opened, gourmet clubs in Dallas and Houston chartered buses to Austin just to shop at Central Market. They called their trips "pilgrimages." Now those cities have their own Central Markets.

One zealous couple organized an informal grassroots campaign to persuade us to open a Fort Worth store. They wrote letters to Charles Butt and John Campbell, clipped real estate ads and mailed news articles that might help the cause. Friends joined the crusade, and the store in Fort Worth was finally built on a piece of property located by Fort Worth customers.

Lamb Mechada

6 garlic cloves

2 tablespoons chopped fresh marjoram leaves

1 teaspoon salt

3 tablespoons lime juice

1/2 teaspoon Tabasco sauce

3 slices lean smoked bacon

1 (4 1/2- to 5-pound) boneless leg of lamb

30 small pimiento-stuffed green olives

SERVES 10 TO 12

Mash the garlic with the marjoram and salt in a small bowl. Stir in the lime juice and Tabasco sauce. Cut the bacon crosswise into 1/2-inch pieces. Make 15 deep slits over all sides of the lamb. Enlarge each slit with the handle of a wooden spoon. Place 1 green olive, 1 piece of bacon, 1/2 teaspoon of the garlic mixture and a second olive into each slit. Rub any remaining garlic mixture over the lamb.

Position the oven rack in the lower half of a 325-degree oven. Place the lamb fat side up on a rack in a roasting pan; insert a meat thermometer into the thickest portion of the lamb. Roast for 30 minutes for each pound or to 145 degrees on the meat thermometer for medium; roast for 40 minutes for each pound or to 165 degrees for well done.

Remove to a serving platter and let stand for 10 minutes. Slice to serve.

Pairing wines with food can be tricky when there are lots of contrasting flavors. Zinfandel is a classic pairing for lamb, but the recipe for Lamb Mechada throws us a few curve balls like briny green olives, sour lime juice and hot Tabasco sauce.

Our Central Market wine steward agreed that Zinfandel would be a good choice, but advised us to look for one that's a bit fruity and spicy, not dry. Other good choices would be a California Syrah or Australian Shiraz or a Nero d'Avola from Sicily. White wine devotees may want to consider a Fallegro from Spain or an Encruzado from Portugal.

Rack of Lamb with Pistachio Mint Pesto

1 cup unsalted pistachios,
lightly toasted

1 1/2 cups packed mint leaves,
about 2 large bunches

1 cup packed stemmed
spinach leaves

1/2 cup (2 ounces) freshly grated
Parmesan cheese

2 tablespoons lime juice

1 1/2 teaspoons kosher salt

1/2 teaspoon cayenne pepper

1/4 teaspoon freshly ground
white pepper

1 cup olive oil

2 (8- or 9-rib) lamb racks

SERVES 4

Process the pistachios in a food processor until finely ground. Add the mint, spinach, Parmesan cheese, lime juice, kosher salt, cayenne pepper and white pepper. Process to form a coarse paste. Drizzle in the olive oil gradually, processing constantly to form a smooth paste.

Ask the butcher to trim the fat and the tail from the lamb racks, leaving only a thin layer of fat, and to French the ribs, leaving only the eye of the rack with the bones attached. Heat a large skillet until very hot. Place the lamb fat side down in the skillet and sear on both sides. Stand the racks on end with tongs and sear both ends; the racks should be brown on all sides, but still rare in the center. Cool to room temperature. Chill in the refrigerator. Let stand at room temperature for 15 minutes before roasting.

Spread the pistachio mixture generously over the underside of the lamb; do not spread on the bones. Turn the racks over and place on a rack in a shallow roasting pan; spread with the remaining pistachio mixture. Insert a meat thermometer into the thickest portion of the lamb without touching a bone.

Position the oven rack in the center of a 450-degree oven. Roast the lamb for 15 minutes or to 120 degrees on the meat thermometer for rare. Roast to 130 degrees for medium or to 140 degrees for well done; the pesto coating will become darker as the lamb roasts.

Remove the lamb to a cutting board and let stand for 5 minutes. Carve into double chops to serve. Allow 2 double chops for each serving.

Chipotle-Rubbed Pork Tenderloin with Mango-Blueberry Salsa

Pork Tenderloin

4 canned chipotle chiles in adobo

1 tablespoon olive oil

3 tablespoons honey

1 teaspoon salt

1/2 teaspoon freshly ground pepper

2 pork tenderloins, trimmed

Mango-Blueberry Salsa

1 cup chopped mango, about 1 small mango

2 teaspoons minced seeded fresh serrano chile

1/2 cup finely chopped red onion

1/2 cup finely chopped red bell pepper

1/2 cup cilantro leaves, chopped

1/4 cup seasoned rice vinegar

1/4 teaspoon freshly ground pepper

1 cup fresh blueberries

salt to taste

SERVES 6

For the pork, remove and discard the stems and seeds of the chiles. Combine the chiles with the olive oil, honey, salt and pepper in a blender and process until puréed. Rub the chile mixture over the pork tenderloins, wearing rubber gloves. Marinate in the refrigerator for 3 hours.

For the salsa, combine the mango, chile, onion, bell pepper and cilantro in a bowl. Add the vinegar and pepper and mix well. Fold in the blueberries. Season with salt. Let stand for 1 hour.

To roast the pork, position the oven rack in the center of a 425-degree oven. Place the pork on a rack in a shallow roasting pan, tucking under the thinner ends to ensure uniform thickness. Insert a meat thermometer into the thickest portion of the pork. Roast for 20 to 25 minutes or to 155 degrees on the meat thermometer.

Remove the pork to a cutting board and let stand for 5 minutes. Carve into 1/2-inch slices and serve with the salsa.

CM carries a Southwestern-flavor marinated pork tenderloin in the meat market. As a timesaver, you can start with that and eliminate the chipotle rub.

Pork Chops Stuffed with Apple, Raisins and Pecans

1 Empire, Gravenstein or Russet apple, peeled and chopped

1/2 cup golden raisins

1/4 cup currants

2 teaspoons finely minced fresh sage

2 teaspoons olive oil

1 (12-ounce) can frozen apple juice concentrate, thawed

1/2 cup maple-roasted pecans, coarsely chopped

1/4 teaspoon salt

4 double-thick pork chops

salt and pepper to taste

1 tablespoon olive oil

1/4 cup water

SERVES 4

Combine the apple, raisins, currants, sage, 2 teaspoons olive oil and 1/2 cup of the apple juice concentrate in a small saucepan. Bring to a boil and reduce the heat. Simmer for 5 minutes or until the fruit is plumped and the mixture thickens. Stir in the pecans and 1/4 teaspoon salt. Cool slightly.

Cut a pocket 21/2 inches deep and 3 inches wide in each pork chop, cutting to the bone. Season generously on both sides with salt and pepper to taste. Spoon the stuffing into the pockets and close the pockets with wooden picks.

Heat 1 tablespoon olive oil in a large ovenproof skillet over medium-high heat. Add the pork chops and cook until golden brown on both sides. Mix the remaining apple juice concentrate with the water in a bowl and pour over the chops.

Bake at 375 degrees for 30 minutes, basting occasionally with the pan juices. Let stand for 10 minutes. Remove the wooden picks and spoon the pan juices over the chops to serve.

You may use almost any kind of dried fruit for this recipe, including dried plums, apricots, cherries and cranberries.

Pork Chops with Rosemary, Lemon and Olives

2 boneless pork chops, butterflied

1/3 cup flour

1/2 teaspoon salt

1/4 teaspoon pepper

3 tablespoons olive oil

3 tablespoons minced fresh
rosemary leaves

3 garlic cloves, minced

1/3 cup dry sherry or white wine

1/2 cup sliced kalamata olives

juice of 1 lemon

1/2 cup chicken stock

salt and pepper to taste

lemon slices and rosemary sprigs

SERVES 2

Pound the pork chops to flatten slightly. Mix the flour, 1/2 teaspoon salt and 1/4 teaspoon pepper together. Coat the pork chops on both sides with the flour mixture. Heat half the olive oil in a skillet over medium heat. Add the pork chops and sauté for 5 to 6 minutes on each side or until cooked through. Remove to a platter and cover to keep warm.

Add the remaining olive oil to the skillet and add the rosemary and garlic. Sauté for 1 minute.

Stir in the wine and cook until reduced by half. Add the olives, lemon juice and chicken stock. Simmer for 3 minutes. Season with salt and pepper to taste.

Return the pork chops to the skillet and cook until heated through. Spoon the sauce over the chops to serve and garnish with lemon slices and rosemary sprigs.

Pork is the perfect meat for an adventurous cook. At Central Market, we especially like Berkshire pork. That's not a brand—it's a specific breed of hog that's rich, moist, beautifully marbled and tender. Ours is raised on several small Iowa farms, in strict compliance with the U.S.D.A.'s certified "All Natural" program, given no hormones and fed an all-vegetable diet. Berkshire pork's robust flavor allows it to stand up to the vivid flavors of many different cuisines.

Pork and Apple Chili

4 1/2 tablespoons corn oil

3 pounds pork loin, cut into
1/2-inch cubes

1 1/2 tablespoons
Cajun seasoning

1 red onion, coarsely chopped

2 large garlic cloves, minced

1 large red bell pepper,
coarsely chopped

1 jalapeño chile, seeded
and minced

3 cups beef stock or beef broth

2 (28-ounce) cans peeled
tomatoes, drained and
coarsely chopped

3 Granny Smith apples, peeled
and coarsely chopped

3 bay leaves

1 1/2 tablespoons light
brown sugar

1 1/2 teaspoons chili powder

2 (15-ounce) cans kidney beans,
drained and rinsed

kosher salt to taste

SERVES 8 TO 10

Heat the corn oil in a large heavy saucepan over high heat. Combine the pork with the Cajun seasoning in a large bowl and toss to coat well. Add the pork to the saucepan in batches and cook for 2 to 3 minutes or until brown on all sides. Remove the batches to a bowl.

Add the onion, garlic, bell pepper and chile to the saucepan and sauté for 2 minutes or until tender. Stir in the beef stock and tomatoes. Bring to a boil, stirring up the browned bits from the bottom of the saucepan. Reduce the heat and simmer for 5 minutes.

Add the apples, bay leaves, brown sugar and chili powder. Simmer for 30 minutes or until the apples are tender. Stir in the beans and browned pork along with any accumulated juices.

Simmer for 10 to 15 minutes or until the pork is cooked through. Season with kosher salt. Remove and discard the bay leaves. Ladle the chili into bowls to serve.

$\mathcal{CM}$ carries beans of all varieties in both the Bulk Foods department and the Specialty Foods department. You may want to sample anasazi, scarlet runner, tongues of fire, black turtle or calypso beans.

Country Cassoulet

2 cups dried Great Northern beans

2 cups dried small white lima beans

1 duck

2 large onions, cut into 1/2-inch pieces

1 tablespoon olive oil

8 ounces thick-cut smoked bacon, cut into 2-inch pieces

2 quarts chicken stock

1 pound boneless pork, cut into 2-inch pieces

10 garlic cloves, minced

3 tablespoons tomato paste

4 teaspoons chopped fresh thyme

1 1/2 teaspoons salt

1/2 teaspoon pepper

1 quart chicken stock

2 1/2 cups dry white wine

1 pound andouille sausage, cut into 1 1/2-inch pieces

1 cup fresh bread crumbs

1 tablespoon butter, melted

SERVES 8 TO 10

Sort and rinse the beans. Combine with enough water to cover in a large saucepan and soak for 8 to 12 hours.

Combine the duck and 1/2 cup of the onions with enough water to cover in a large saucepan. Simmer for 1 hour; drain, reserving the liquid. Cool and bone the duck. Skim and reserve 1 tablespoon of the duck drippings from the liquid, discarding the remaining drippings and liquid. Drain the beans.

Heat the olive oil in a large saucepan over medium heat. Add the bacon and sauté for 2 minutes. Stir in 2 quarts chicken stock and the beans. Simmer, covered, for 1 hour or until the beans are almost tender. Drain, reserving the liquid.

Heat the reserved duck drippings in a large Dutch oven. Add the pork and cook for 3 minutes or until brown on all sides; drain. Stir in the remaining onions, garlic, tomato paste, thyme, salt and pepper. Add 1 quart chicken stock and the wine.

Cover the Dutch oven and bring to a boil. Place in a 350-degree oven and bake for 30 minutes.

Brown the sausage in a skillet. Add to the Dutch oven with the beans and duck. Bake for 30 minutes, adding the reserved bean liquid as needed.

Mix the bread crumbs and melted butter in a bowl. Sprinkle over the cassoulet. Bake for 15 to 20 minutes longer or until the bread crumbs are golden brown.

Pasta, salad and bread are the perfect fast food, and Americans have adopted this Mediterranean trio as their own. But the whole can't be greater that the sum of its parts, so don't skimp on your salad.

The day Central Market opened, we devoted a 6×8-foot ice bank to a display of head lettuce—a regiment of round, green, leafy bowling balls. Over the course of that first frantic day, we sold out of mesclun, arugula, butter lettuce, frisée—all the wild, butter and fancy lettuces were carted away by excited customers.

When the store closed, the head lettuce was still there. We knew then that you, our fellow food-lovers—had found us and that our little experiment—Central Market—was going to be successful.

Pasta Tre Colore

2 tablespoons olive oil

4 ounces prosciutto, or 8 ounces smoked ham, chopped

3 garlic cloves, minced

2 tablespoons unsalted butter

1 1/2 cups heavy cream

1 cup baby peas

1 cup packed basil leaves, chopped

12 ounces refrigerated fresh fettucini

1 cup (4 ounces) grated Parmigiano-Reggiano cheese

freshly ground pepper to taste

SERVES 4

Heat the olive oil in a large sauté pan over medium heat. Add the prosciutto and sauté until brown, stirring occasionally. Reduce the heat to medium-low and add the garlic. Sauté for 1 minute. Stir in the butter, cream, peas and basil. Cook until slightly thickened; keep warm.

Cook the pasta using the package directions; drain. Stir the cheese into the sauce and add the hot pasta, tossing to coat well; add additional cream if needed for the desired consistency. Season with pepper and serve immediately.

Savory Breakfast Patties

1 pound lean ground beef

1 pound ground veal

1 pound ground pork

4 garlic cloves, minced

1 bunch scallions, minced

1 teaspoon chopped fennel

2 teaspoons maple syrup

2 to 3 teaspoons ground cumin,
or to taste

1 teaspoon thyme

1 teaspoon sage

1/2 teaspoon ginger

2 pinches of nutmeg

2 teaspoons salt

crushed red pepper flakes to taste

2 teaspoons black pepper

butter

SERVES 14

Combine the ground beef, ground veal and ground pork in a large bowl. Add the garlic, scallions, fennel, maple syrup, cumin, thyme, sage, ginger, nutmeg, salt, red pepper flakes and black pepper. Mix well with a spoon or moistened hands.

Shape the mixture into two 7-inch logs, 2 inches in diameter. Wrap in waxed paper and chill in the refrigerator for 2 hours to 2 days. Slice the logs into 1/2-inch patties.

Melt a small amount of butter in a skillet over medium heat. Add the patties and cook for 3 to 4 minutes on each side or until cooked through.

Obviously, this spicy variation on the country sausage patty is great for breakfast and brunch. But most of us remember those special childhood evenings when Mom served breakfast for supper, and these breakfast patties would be wonderful fare for that kind of easy evening, alongside eggs and biscuits. Because of the sweet touch of maple syrup, they are also especially good with a stack of flapjacks slathered with double-cream butter and real maple syrup.

Sausage and Biscuit Casserole

1 1/2 to 2 pounds mild or hot bulk pork breakfast sausage
1 cup chopped sweet onion
2 cups baking mix
3/4 to 1 cup (3 to 4 ounces) shredded sharp Cheddar cheese
1 cup low-fat buttermilk
1 teaspoon poultry seasoning

SERVES 8 TO 10

Brown the sausage lightly in a skillet, stirring until crumbly. Add the onion and sauté for 4 to 5 minutes or until the onion is translucent. Remove to a 9×13-inch baking dish sprayed with nonstick cooking spray.

Combine the baking mix, cheese, buttermilk and poultry seasoning in a medium bowl and mix well to form a sticky dough. Drop by tablespoonfuls onto the sausage mixture. Bake at 425 degrees for 20 minutes or until the biscuits are light brown.

You may add cayenne pepper or chili powder and use the hot sausage for a spicier version of this dish.

At Central Market, sausage is a truly creative enterprise. We make about 70 different kinds of sausage, different styles for different seasons: chicken sausage, lamb sausage, pork sausage, beef sausage, sausages with Cheddar cheese, cilantro, spinach, feta. When Texas blueberry season rolls around, we even make a maple-pork-blueberry sausage. Creativity inspires creativity, so we weren't too surprised to hear that one of our butchers, Don, has developed a recipe for blueberry sausage pancakes with the cooked sausage crumbled directly into the batter.

Roast Chicken with Fresh Tarragon

1 (3^{1}/$_{2}$- to 4^{1}/$_{2}$-pound) chicken

1 bunch fresh tarragon

salt and freshly ground pepper to taste

2 carrots, peeled and cut into halves lengthwise

1 small onion, cut into halves

2 tablespoons unsalted butter, softened

^{1}/$_{4}$ cup dry white wine

^{1}/$_{2}$ cup unsalted or low-sodium chicken broth

SERVES 4

Rinse the chicken and pat dry. Separate the skin gently from the breast and thighs of the chicken with the hand and insert several sprigs of tarragon under the skin. Sprinkle with salt and pepper. Tie the legs together with kitchen twine. Place the carrots and onion in a shallow roasting pan and place the chicken breast side up in the pan. Insert a meat thermometer into the thickest portion of the breast without touching the bone.

Roast the chicken at 425 degrees for 20 minutes, basting with butter after 10 minutes. Turn the chicken onto the side and baste with butter. Roast for 10 minutes. Turn the chicken onto the other side and baste with butter. Roast for 10 minutes. Turn the chicken breast side up and roast for 1 hour longer or to 170 degrees on the meat thermometer and the juices run clear, basting every 10 minutes with the pan juices.

Place the chicken on a cutting board and cover loosely with foil. Let stand for 10 minutes. Discard the vegetables in the roasting pan and skim the fat from the cooking juices. Place the pan over high heat. Add the wine and stir to scrape any browned bits from the bottom of the pan. Stir in the chicken broth. Cook until the sauce is reduced enough to lightly coat the spoon, stirring occasionally. Strain the sauce into a bowl.

Cut the chicken into serving pieces. Drizzle with the strained sauce. Garnish with chopped fresh tarragon.

Oven-Roasted Cornish Hens with Dried Fruit Couscous

Cornish Hens

4 Cornish hens

1 small onion, cut into quarters

salt and pepper to taste

2 tablespoons butter, melted

1/2 cup apricot preserves

1 tablespoon Dijon mustard

1 teaspoon grated gingerroot, or 1/2 teaspoon ground ginger

Dried Fruit Couscous

1/3 cup golden raisins

2/3 cup chopped dried apricots

2/3 cup dried fruit tidbits

2 cups chicken stock

3 tablespoons butter

1 teaspoon salt

1 1/2 cups uncooked couscous

1/2 cup toasted slivered almonds

1/2 teaspoon ground coriander

SERVES 4

For the hens, rinse under cold running water, drain and pat dry. Tuck the wing tips behind the breast and place 1/4 onion in the cavity of each. Sprinkle inside and out with salt and pepper and tie the legs together with kitchen twine. Place on a rack in a roasting pan and brush with the melted butter.

Roast the hens at 325 degrees for 45 minutes. Melt the preserves in a saucepan. Stir in the Dijon mustard and gingerroot. Brush over the hens and roast for 30 to 45 minutes longer or until the juices run clear when pierced with a fork; brush occasionally with the remaining preserve mixture.

For the couscous, combine the raisins, apricots and fruit tidbits with enough water to cover in a large saucepan. Bring to a boil and reduce the heat. Simmer for 2 minutes. Let stand for 10 minutes; drain.

Combine the chicken stock, butter and salt in a large saucepan and bring to a boil. Stir in the couscous, fruit mixture, almonds and coriander. Cover and remove from the heat. Let stand for 10 minutes. Fluff with a fork and serve with the hens.

Citrus-Glazed Roast Duck with Texas Grapefruit Chutney

Texas Grapefruit Chutney

1/2 cup cider vinegar

3/4 cup sugar

1/2 cup packed brown sugar

1/2 cup grapefruit juice

1/4 teaspoon freshly grated nutmeg

1/2 teaspoon sea salt

1/3 cup dried cranberries

1/3 cup golden raisins

1/3 cup currants

1 large jalapeño chile, seeded and minced

1 Texas grapefruit, sectioned and chopped

1/2 cup coarsely chopped sweet onion

4 large garlic cloves, chopped

2 tablespoons grated gingerroot

Duck

2 tablespoons white wine vinegar

2 tablespoons sugar

2 tablespoons grated grapefruit zest

1/2 cup Texas Red grapefruit juice

1 tablespoon lemon juice

2 tablespoons brandy or cognac

4 (6- to 7-ounce) boneless duck breasts

1 teaspoon sea salt

SERVES 4

For the chutney, combine the vinegar, sugar, brown sugar, grapefruit juice, nutmeg and sea salt in a heavy saucepan. Bring to a boil over medium heat. Add the cranberries, raisins, currants, chile, grapefruit, onion, garlic and gingerroot. Reduce the heat and simmer for 20 minutes or until thickened. Let stand until cool.

For the duck, combine the vinegar, sugar, grapefruit zest, grapefruit juice and lemon juice in a small saucepan. Bring to a boil over medium heat. Remove from the heat and stir in the brandy.

Rub the duck with the sea salt and brush with the grapefruit glaze. Cook skin side down in a heavy skillet over medium heat for 2 1/2 to 3 minutes or until light brown. Place on a rack in a heavy roasting pan. Insert a meat thermometer into the thickest portion of 1 of the duck breasts.

Place the duck in an oven preheated to 450 degrees and reduce the oven temperature to 375 degrees. Roast for 30 to 40 minutes or to 165 degrees on the meat thermometer, basting with the pan juices and glaze every 7 minutes. Serve with the chutney.

Tortellini with Smoked Turkey and Mozzarella

1 (9-ounce) package fresh cheese tortellini

olive oil

1 tablespoon butter

1 tablespoon minced garlic

1/2 cup dry white wine

8 ounces asparagus, trimmed and cut into 1-inch pieces

1/2 cup sliced fresh mushrooms

1 cup half-and-half or heavy cream

1 smoked turkey leg, skinned, boned and chopped

salt and pepper to taste

1/2 cup (2 ounces) shredded smoked mozzarella or provolone cheese

2 tablespoons chopped fresh basil leaves

1 tablespoon chopped fresh oregano leaves

SERVES 4

Cook the pasta using the package directions; drain. Toss the hot pasta with a small amount of olive oil in a bowl.

Melt the butter in a large sauté pan. Add the garlic and sauté for 1 minute. Add the wine, asparagus and mushrooms. Cook until the vegetables are tender and the wine evaporates, stirring occasionally. Stir in the half-and-half and turkey. Bring to a simmer and cook for 5 minutes or until reduced by half. Remove from the heat and season with salt and pepper.

Add the pasta to the sauce and toss to coat well. Spoon into a large pasta bowl or platter. Sprinkle with the cheese, basil and oregano. Serve immediately.

Texas Gulf Flounder with Herb Crust

6 (4- to 6-ounce) flounder fillets or other thin fillets

1 tablespoon olive oil

salt and freshly ground pepper to taste

1/4 cup finely chopped mixed herbs

1/2 cup Japanese panko bread crumbs

3 tablespoons olive oil

SERVES 4 TO 6

Brush the fish fillets with 1 tablespoon olive oil and season on both sides with salt and pepper. Mix the fresh herbs with the bread crumbs in a shallow dish. Coat the fish fillets on both sides with the crumb mixture, pressing to adhere.

Heat 3 tablespoons olive oil in an ovenproof skillet. Add the fish and sauté for 2 minutes on each side or until golden brown. Bake at 400 degrees for 3 to 5 minutes.

Blackened Red Snapper

1 tablespoon paprika

1 teaspoon onion powder

1 teaspoon garlic powder

1/2 teaspoon dried thyme, finely crumbled

1/2 teaspoon dried oregano, finely crumbled

1/2 teaspoon salt

1/2 teaspoon black pepper

1/2 teaspoon white pepper

1/4 teaspoon cayenne pepper

4 (4- to 6-ounce) red snapper fillets

1/4 cup (1/2 stick) butter, melted

SERVES 4

Combine the paprika, onion powder, garlic powder, thyme, oregano, salt, black pepper, white pepper and cayenne pepper in a shallow dish. Dip the fish fillets into the melted butter, then into the seasoning mixture.

Heat a cast-iron skillet until very hot and add the fish. Cook for 2 minutes on each side or until blackened.

Sear-Roasted Salmon Fillets with Citrus-Ginger Butter

Citrus-Ginger Butter

1¹/2 teaspoons fresh lemon juice

1¹/2 teaspoons fresh orange juice

1 green onion, trimmed and finely minced

2 tablespoons finely grated gingerroot

6 tablespoons (³/4 stick) butter, softened

Salmon

3 tablespoons dry bread crumbs

2 tablespoons minced fresh parsley

1 green onion, trimmed and finely minced

grated zest of ¹/2 orange

¹/4 teaspoon garlic salt

4 (6- to 8-ounce) skinless salmon fillets

3 tablespoons olive oil

SERVES 4

For the butter, combine the lemon juice, orange juice, green onion, gingerroot and butter in a bowl and beat until smooth. Shape into a log 1¹/2 inches in diameter on a piece of plastic wrap. Wrap tightly, twisting the ends. Chill in the refrigerator.

For the salmon, mix the bread crumbs with the parsley, green onion, orange zest and garlic salt in a shallow dish. Coat the inner side of the fish fillets with the crumb mixture.

Heat the olive oil in a large ovenproof skillet over medium-high heat until it shimmers. Add the fish fillets crumb side down and cook for 1 minute or until that side is brown. Remove the skillet from the heat and turn the fillets crumb side up.

Roast the fish at 450 degrees for 5 to 7 minutes or until the thickest portion flakes easily with a fork. Place on a platter. Cut the butter into rounds and place 1 or 2 rounds on each fish fillet.

Sautéed Fish with Coconut and Lime Sauce

Fish

1/2 cup flour

1/2 teaspoon salt

1/4 teaspoon freshly ground pepper

4 (6-ounce) pieces mild firm fish, such as opah, mahi mahi or snapper

2 tablespoons vegetable oil

Coconut and Lime Sauce

2 stalks lemon grass (optional)

1 cup canned coconut milk

3 tablespoons freshly squeezed lime juice

1/2 teaspoon grated lime zest

8 thin slices peeled gingerroot

1 serrano chile, thinly sliced into rounds

1 teaspoon salt

SERVES 4

For the fish, mix the flour, salt and pepper in a shallow dish. Coat the fish with the flour mixture, shaking to remove the excess. Heat the oil in a skillet over medium-high heat. Add the fish and sauté until golden brown on both sides. Remove to a plate and cover with foil to keep warm.

For the sauce, wipe out the skillet used for the fish. Peel the lemon grass and trim to the white portion. Bruise the white portions of the stalks with the back of a knife. Combine with the coconut milk, lime juice, lime zest, gingerroot, chile and salt in the skillet. Bring to a boil, stirring frequently. Boil for 5 minutes or until slightly reduced and the flavors blend, stirring occasionally.

Add the fish gently to the sauce. Reduce the heat and simmer for 2 minutes. Remove and discard the lemon grass. Serve with hot steamed rice.

Pasta with Lobster, Rapini and Radicchio

1 large bunch rapini,
stems removed

8 ounces long pasta

3 large garlic cloves, thinly sliced

2 teaspoons crushed red
pepper flakes

6 tablespoons olive oil

meat of 2 lobster tails,
coarsely chopped

1 small head radicchio, chopped

2 tablespoons olive oil

1$1/2$ teaspoons sea salt

$1/4$ teaspoon pepper

SERVES 8

Combine the rapini with enough water to cover in a bowl and let stand for 3 minutes or longer; drain. Cook the pasta al dente in enough water to cover in a large saucepan; drain.

Sauté the garlic and red pepper flakes in 6 tablespoons olive oil in a deep skillet over medium heat. Add the lobster and sauté until the

lobster turns red. Remove the lobster mixture to a bowl and cover with foil to keep warm.

Add the rapini and radicchio to the skillet. Cook, covered, for 1 minute or until the rapini is wilted. Add the pasta, lobster mixture, 2 tablespoons olive oil, sea salt and pepper; toss to mix well. Serve warm in a heated bowl.

CM carries rapini, a typically Tuscan vegetable. It has a pungent flavor somewhat like a turnip green and can be fried, stewed, steamed or braised. It may also be called broccolirab or broccoli rabe.

Seared Scallops with Leeks

16 large sea scallops, about 1 1/2 pounds

salt and pepper to taste

2 large leeks

3 tablespoons unsalted butter

1/2 cup dry white wine

1/2 cup clam juice

1 tablespoon fresh lemon juice

1/4 cup heavy cream

1 tablespoon minced fresh chives

SERVES 4

Rinse the scallops under cold water. Drain and pat dry. Season on all sides with salt and pepper.

Remove and discard the dark green portions and 1/2 inch of the root ends of the leeks. Cut the leek bulbs into halves lengthwise and then crosswise into 1/4-inch slices. Soak in a large bowl of cold water to remove sand and then remove with a slotted spoon.

Heat the butter in a skillet over medium heat until the foam subsides. Add the scallops and sear for 5 minutes or until golden brown on all sides. Remove to an ovenproof plate and keep warm in a 300-degree oven.

Add the leeks to the skillet and sauté until tender and golden brown. Add the wine and cook until the wine has nearly evaporated. Stir in the clam juice and lemon juice. Cook until reduced by half. Add the cream and bring just to a low boil; cook for 1 minute. Remove from the heat and add the chives; season with salt and pepper.

Spoon the scallops onto 4 serving plates and spoon the sauce over the top to serve.

This recipe will serve 6 as an appetizer.

Seafood Cannelloni with Tomato Cream Sauce

Tomato Cream Sauce

3 tablespoons olive oil

1 cup chopped onion

2 garlic cloves, chopped

2 pounds fresh tomatoes
or drained canned
tomatoes, chopped

1/2 teaspoon red pepper flakes

salt and black pepper to taste

1/4 cup chopped fresh basil

2 tablespoons chopped fresh
Italian parsley

2 tablespoons vodka

3/4 cup heavy cream

Cannelloni

1 cup sliced leeks

2 garlic cloves, minced

3 tablespoons olive oil

8 ounces scallops

8 ounces shrimp, peeled,
deveined and coarsely chopped

8 ounces lump crabmeat

3 tablespoons chopped
fresh basil

1 tablespoon chopped
fresh oregano

1/4 teaspoon red pepper flakes

16 ounces ricotta cheese

1 1/2 cups (6 ounces) shredded
provolone cheese

1 1/2 cups (6 ounces) shredded
mozzarella cheese

1/2 cup (2 ounces) grated
Parmigiano-Reggiano cheese

1 egg, beaten

salt and pepper to taste

16 (3- to 4-inch-wide) sheets
fresh pasta, cooked, drained
and cooled

SERVES 8

For the sauce, heat the olive oil in a saucepan. Add the onion and garlic and sauté until tender. Add the tomatoes and cook for 20 minutes. Season with red pepper flakes, salt and black pepper.

Purée in a food processor or blender and return to the saucepan. Add the basil, parsley, vodka and cream. Simmer for 10 minutes. Adjust the seasonings.

For the cannelloni, sauté the leeks and garlic in the olive oil in a saucepan until tender. Add the scallops, shrimp and crabmeat and sauté for 3 minutes. Stir in the basil, oregano and red pepper flakes. Cool to room temperature.

Combine the cheeses in a large bowl. Add the egg and season with salt and pepper. Stir in the seafood mixture.

Spread 1 cup of the tomato cream sauce in a buttered 9×13-inch baking dish. Spread about 1/3 cup of the seafood filling on each pasta sheet and roll to enclose the filling.

Place seam side down in the prepared baking dish. Pour the remaining sauce over the top. Cover the dish with foil and bake at 350 degrees for 45 minutes.

Seaport Paella

2 tablespoons vegetable oil or peanut oil

12 ounces Cajun Hollar Inc. Smoked Cajun Style Andouille Sausage, chopped

1 large onion, finely chopped

4 large garlic cloves, minced

1 large green bell pepper, chopped

1 large red bell pepper, chopped

1 teaspoon Spanish saffron threads

1 cup white wine

2 1/2 quarts chicken stock or chicken broth

1 cup uncooked long grain rice

salt and pepper to taste

2 boneless skinless chicken breasts, cut into 1-inch pieces

1 pound medium shrimp, peeled and deveined

1 pound bay scallops

2 pounds mussels, scrubbed and debearded

SERVES 8 TO 10

Heat the oil in a stockpot or Dutch oven over medium-high heat until hot but not smoking. Add the sausage and sauté until brown around the edges. Add the onion and garlic and sauté for 3 minutes or until the onion is tender. Add the bell peppers and saffron and sauté for 3 minutes.

Add the wine and stir to loosen the browned bits from the bottom of the stockpot. Stir in the chicken stock. Bring to a simmer and simmer for 20 to 30 minutes or until the flavors blend. Stir in the rice and cook until the rice is tender. Season with salt and pepper.

Add the chicken, shrimp, scallops and mussels. Bring to a simmer and simmer until the chicken is cooked through and the mussels open; remove any mussels that do not open. Serve immediately in bowls.

You may substitute other sausage for the andouille sausage suggested, but it must be fully cooked or smoked.

Enchiladas de Huevos Verano

Enchilada Sauce

1 to 3 garlic cloves, minced

3 scallions, finely chopped

2 serrano or jalapeño chiles, seeded and chopped, or to taste

1 tablespoon canola oil or peanut oil

1 (8-ounce) can tomato sauce

1 cup chicken stock

salt and pepper to taste

Enchiladas

canola oil

12 corn tortillas

6 eggs, beaten

2 cups shredded iceberg lettuce

2 avocados, sliced

1 red onion, thinly sliced

6 radishes, thinly sliced

1 Roma tomato, chopped

SERVES 4

For the sauce, sauté the garlic, scallions and chiles in the canola oil in a skillet until the scallions are translucent. Add the tomato sauce and chicken stock; season with salt and pepper. Simmer until the sauce thickens.

For the enchiladas, heat enough canola oil to cover the bottom of a skillet until it sizzles when a tortilla is added. Add the tortillas 1 at a time and cook just until heated through; remove to paper towels to drain and keep warm.

Cook the eggs in a nonstick skillet until soft scrambled. Spoon onto the tortillas and spoon some of the sauce over the eggs. Roll the tortillas to enclose the filling and arrange 3 on each serving plate. Spoon the remaining sauce over the enchiladas.

Top with the lettuce, avocado, onion, radishes and tomato in the order listed and serve immediately.

Scrambled Eggs Supreme

1 teaspoon light chili powder

1/4 teaspoon ground cumin

1/4 teaspoon dried oregano leaves

8 eggs

1/4 cup cottage cheese

1/3 cup buttermilk

1/2 teaspoon Worcestershire sauce

1/2 teaspoon Tabasco sauce

1/2 cup (2 ounces) shredded Black Diamond Extra Old White Canadian Cheddar Cheese

1/4 teaspoon garlic salt

1/4 teaspoon pepper

salt to taste

4 portobello mushroom caps

1 tablespoon olive oil

SERVES 4

Combine the chili powder, cumin and oregano in a small bowl and mix well to crush the oregano leaves. Combine 1/2 teaspoon of the mixture with the eggs in a bowl. Add the cottage cheese, buttermilk, Worcestershire sauce, Tabasco sauce, cheese, garlic salt and pepper. Stir just until mixed.

Spoon into a nonstick skillet and cook just until soft scrambled, stirring frequently. Season with salt to taste.

Brush the mushroom caps with the olive oil and arrange on a baking sheet. Bake at 350 degrees for 3 to 5 minutes or until heated through. Spoon the egg mixture into the mushroom caps and sprinkle lightly with the remaining chili powder mixture.

Many Central Market Partners have trained at culinary schools and in restaurant kitchens; others have spent their lives in the grocery business. Our Cooking School Coordinator is an honors graduate of the Culinary Institute of America. But some have followed less-than-direct paths to get here. Two Partners were professional ballet dancers, and others had full careers as doctors and lawyers. There are plenty of musicians in our midst, several retired executives and at least one former television news anchor. They all got hooked on cooking in their own home kitchens, many of them starting out with variations on that most adaptable of dishes, scrambled eggs.

COMPLEMENTS

Vegetables
Side Dishes
Breads
Beverages

Central Market's produce never fails to awe first-timers;
most people have never seen such an incredible array of fruits and
vegetables, and few produce departments elicit the simple
question, "What is it?" as often as the one at Central Market.
It's enough to make anyone consider vegetarianism
(until you turn the corner into the meat and fish departments).
In Nashville, where we shot the photographs for this book
and for our quarterly magazine, Foodie, the studio crew often
breaks for a lunch in traditional Southern style,
ordering "meat and three" from a tiny, country-cooking
institution called Arnold's around the corner.
Often, though, we find ourselves ordering just "three"
without the meat because, Dr. Atkins aside, the American diet
has shifted in the last decades.
The truth is, the dishes we used to call "sides"
are now front and center.

both sides, removing the slices to the baking sheet as they brown. Pour the oil out of the skillet and wipe out the skillet if the bread crumbs begin to burn; add additional oil to continue. Bake the slices at 350 degrees for 15 minutes or until tender. Reduce the oven temperature to 300 degrees. Cool the eggplant to room temperature.

Oil a baking pan lightly with olive oil. Spread the ricotta mixture over 2/3 of the eggplant slices.

Arrange uniform stacks of 2 spread eggplant slices in the pan and top the stacks with the remaining plain eggplant slices.

Spoon about 1/3 cup marinara sauce onto each stack, allowing it to drip down the sides; sprinkle the mozzarella cheese over the tops. Bake for 15 to 20 minutes or until heated through. Serve with additional warm marinara sauce if desired.

Braised Fennel au Gruyère

2 fresh fennel bulbs with leaves
1 quart chicken stock or vegetable stock
1 cup (4 ounces) shredded Gruyère cheese
freshly ground nutmeg to taste
freshly ground pepper to taste

SERVES 4

Cut off the fennel stems and leaves 1 to 2 inches above the bulb; reserve and chop some of the leaves for garnish. Stand the bulb on end and cut into halves lengthwise. Arrange cut side down in a sauté pan. Add enough chicken stock to cover. Simmer, covered, for 15 to 20 minutes or until tender-crisp; drain.

Slice the bulbs diagonally into 1/4-inch slices and arrange in a single layer in a baking dish. Sprinkle with the cheese. Broil in a preheated broiler for 3 to 5 minutes or until the cheese melts and begins to brown.

Sprinkle with nutmeg and the reserved chopped fennel leaves. Serve immediately with freshly ground pepper.

CM recommends the distinct sweet anise flavor of fennel as a perfect complement to many main dishes. It can also be served in salads and grilled.

Fingerling Potatoes with Shiitake Mushrooms

2 pounds fingerling potatoes

8 ounces shiitake mushroom caps, cut into quarters

1 shallot, chopped

1 cup beef broth

3 tablespoons unsalted butter, melted

2 tablespoons plus 1/2 teaspoon sea salt

coarsely ground pepper to taste

SERVES 8

Bring enough water to cover the potatoes to a boil in a large saucepan. Add the potatoes and cook just until they can be pierced with a skewer or knife; do not overcook; drain.

Combine the potatoes with the mushrooms, shallot, beef broth, butter, sea salt and pepper in a roasting pan. Roast at 375 degrees for 30 to 35 minutes or until tender.

You may substitute the drippings from a beef roast for some or all of the beef broth when serving this dish with a roast.

CM stocks several varieties of fingerling potatoes. The Ruby Crescent potato is a classic European fingerling with a slender shape, rose-colored skin and smooth, firm, yellow flesh. Its moist texture makes it a terrific roasting potato. The Russian Fingerling potato is a yellow-skinned banana-shaped potato developed in the Baltic states. It has a firm texture and is great for roasting or for potato salads.

Roasted Potatoes with Fresh Bay Leaves

12 small uniform potatoes

12 fresh bay leaves

1/4 cup olive oil

1 tablespoon chopped fresh rosemary

1 teaspoon sea salt

1 teaspoon pepper

SERVES 6 TO 8

Cut a lengthwise slit in each potato and insert a bay leaf into the slit, leaving a portion of the leaf outside of the potato.

Mix the olive oil, rosemary, sea salt and pepper in a bowl. Add the potatoes and toss to coat evenly. Arrange in a shallow baking dish with the bay leaves up.

Roast at 350 degrees for 45 minutes or until the potatoes are tender and golden brown.

CM potato choices allow you to vary the presentation of potato dishes by using some of the colored varieties. The Purple potato lends an interesting color to mashed potatoes. The Austrian Crescent potato has a light yellow flesh and is delicious boiled, steamed, roasted or baked and topped with sour cream. The Yukon Gold is an all-purpose potato with distinctive yellow flesh and a rich buttery flavor. It is great for boiling, but tends to fall apart if overcooked. Other potatoes have white, red, pink, lavender or blue flesh.

Sherry-Roasted Garlic Mashed Potatoes
with Blue Cheese

Sherry-Roasted Garlic

1/2 cup peeled garlic cloves

1/4 cup dry sherry

2 tablespoons olive oil

Potatoes

2 pounds Yukon Gold potatoes, peeled and cut into 1-inch pieces

6 tablespoons (3/4 stick) butter

1/2 cup (2 ounces) crumbled blue cheese, at room temperature

1 teaspoon (or more) salt

1/3 to 1/2 cup half-and-half, warmed

freshly ground pepper to taste

SERVES 4 TO 6

For the roasted garlic, place the peeled garlic cloves in a baking cup and drizzle with the sherry and olive oil. Cover tightly with foil, crimping the edges tightly to seal. Roast at 325 degrees for 1 1/4 hours or until the garlic is very tender and brown. Cool to room temperature. Mash with the cooking juices to form a smooth paste.

For the potatoes, combine them with enough water to cover in a saucepan and bring to a boil. Reduce the heat and simmer, loosely covered, for 15 to 20 minutes or until the potatoes can be easily pierced with a sharp fork. Drain and return to the saucepan.

Add the butter and mash with a potato masher or beat with a hand mixer until nearly smooth. Add half the garlic mixture, the blue cheese, salt and 1/3 cup half-and-half. Mash or beat until light and fluffy, adding the remaining half-and-half if necessary for the desired consistency. Adjust the seasonings, adding the pepper and additional garlic paste if desired. Serve warm.

Reserve any unused garlic paste for another use, such as the Creamy Fresh Horseradish Mashed Potatoes on page 91.

CM carries the peeled garlic cloves called for in this recipe in the Prepless Produce department.

The main question to ask about an unfamiliar potato is whether it is starchy or waxy. Starchy potatoes like the classic Russet "Idaho" potato bake up light and fluffy, are creamy when mashed and are the best choice for French fries. Just don't wrap them in foil to bake them, as that will trap the moisture and make the potato mushy.

Waxy potatoes like the Red potato are high in moisture and sugar, but low in starch. They hold their shape well and are ideal for roasting or for making soups, stews, casseroles or potato salad. Just don't mash them or you will end up with a sticky, gooey mess.

New potatoes are waxy with a high moisture content and creamy texture. They are especially good steamed or roasted whole a few days after purchase. The medium starch content of the White potato makes it extremely versatile, a great all-purpose potato.

Creamy Fresh Horseradish Mashed Potatoes

2 1/2 pounds potatoes, peeled and coarsely chopped

salt to taste

4 ounces fresh horseradish, peeled and grated

1/4 cup half-and-half

12 ounces cream cheese, softened

1/2 cup (1 stick) unsalted butter

1/2 cup heavy cream

2 tablespoons roasted garlic purée (use Sherry-Roasted Garlic recipe on page 90, omitting the sherry)

white pepper to taste

SERVES 6

Cook the potatoes in enough lightly salted water to cover in a saucepan for 15 minutes or until tender. Whisk the horseradish into the half-and-half in a small bowl.

Drain the potatoes and combine with the cream cheese and butter in a large bowl. Mash until nearly smooth. Add the cream, garlic purée and horseradish mixture and mash until smooth. Season with salt and white pepper.

Tomato Medley with Fresh Corn and Basil

2 tablespoons extra-virgin olive oil

1 tablespoon white wine balsamic vinegar

1^1/2 teaspoons minced shallot

salt and pepper to taste

^{1}/4 cup double-sweet corn kernels

2 pounds tomatoes of different varieties, colors and sizes

12 fresh basil leaves

S E R V E S   4

Whisk the olive oil, balsamic vinegar and shallot together in a bowl. Season with salt and pepper and let stand for 15 minutes. Cook the corn in water to cover in a saucepan for 2 to 3 minutes or until tender; drain. Chill in the refrigerator.

Cut the larger tomatoes into bite-size pieces and the smaller tomatoes into small wedges. Arrange the tomatoes on a serving plate. Sprinkle with the corn and scatter the basil leaves over the top. Drizzle with the olive oil mixture.

CM points out that all tomatoes are not the same. Try the thirty-something varieties of tomatoes in the store—from red to gold to purple and even striped—with exotic names like Cherokee Purple, Green Zebra, Lemon Boy, Pineapple and German Johnson.

Whipped Root Vegetable Swirl

2 pounds Yukon Gold potatoes

8 ounces rutabagas

8 ounces parsnips

1 1/2 pounds carrots

1 (6-ounce) pear

salt to taste

1/8 teaspoon nutmeg

2 tablespoons butter

1/2 cup heavy cream

5 tablespoons butter

pepper to taste

1 tablespoon butter

nutmeg

SERVES 8 TO 10

Peel the potatoes, rutabagas, parsnips, carrots and pear. Cut the potatoes and rutabagas into 2-inch pieces and the parsnips, carrots and pear into 1-inch pieces. Bring 2 large saucepans of lightly salted water to a boil. Add the carrots to 1 saucepan and the pear and remaining vegetables to the other. Cook for 15 to 20 minutes or until very tender; drain.

Purée the carrots with 1/8 teaspoon nutmeg and 2 tablespoons butter in a food processor. Return the potato mixture to the saucepan and cook over low heat for 1 minute or until the excess moisture evaporates. Add the cream and 5 tablespoons butter to the potato mixture and mash until smooth. Season both mixtures with salt and pepper.

Spread 1/2 cupfuls of the mashed potato mixture and the carrot purée at a time in alternating layers in a buttered 2-quart baking dish. Draw a knife through the layers to marbleize. Melt 1 tablespoon butter in a small saucepan and drizzle over the top. Sprinkle with additional nutmeg.

Cover the baking dish with foil. Bake at 350 degrees for 35 to 45 minutes or until the mixture is heated through.

You may prepare the dish in advance and store in the refrigerator for up to 24 hours before baking.

You never know when or how you're going to touch people's lives. According to Bill, a Central Market veteran who started out in the business when he was 15, bagging groceries, "We do it through food."

We have artists, musicians, psychiatrists, psychologists, ballet dancers, reformed lawyers and a part-time welder working in our stores. But they all share a passion for food with each other and with our customers. Food is so often a labor of love, and eating together an act of love. Smells and tastes can call up precious memories as vividly as a strain of music.

Bill remembers a couple standing in the cheese department, getting all misty-eyed about a romantic memory of Sardinia that wafted over them from the scent of a pungent pecorino.

Gorgonzola Risotto

2 tablespoons olive oil

1/2 cup finely chopped onion

2 cups uncooked arborio rice

1 cup dry white wine

4 cups chicken stock, heated

2 cups (8 ounces) crumbled Gorgonzola cheese, or 1/2 cup (2 ounces) grated Parmesan cheese and 2 teaspoons truffle oil

salt and freshly ground pepper to taste

SERVES 8

Heat the olive oil in a 3-quart saucepan over medium heat. Add the onion and sauté until translucent. Add the rice and sauté until the rice begins to look opaque and the onion begins to brown. Stir in the wine and cook until the wine is absorbed, stirring constantly.

Add 3 cups of the chicken stock and simmer over low heat until the rice is tender, stirring constantly. Stir in the remaining cup of chicken stock and cook until the mixture is creamy, stirring constantly.

Remove from the heat and add the cheese, stirring to melt evenly. Season with the salt and pepper and serve immediately.

This recipe will also serve 4 as a meatless main course.

Wild Rice and Sage Dressing

1 cup pecan halves

2/3 cup uncooked wild rice

2 cups water

1/2 teaspoon salt

6 cups cubed Central Market
Pagnotta, Sourdough or Pain
Francais bread, crusts removed

1/2 cup finely chopped onion
or shallots

4 teaspoons chopped fresh sage

1/2 teaspoon salt

freshly ground pepper to taste

1/2 cup (1 stick) butter, melted

SERVES 6 TO 8

Spread the pecans in a shallow baking pan. Toast at 250 degrees for 10 minutes or until golden brown. Cool slightly and break into pieces.

Rinse the wild rice well. Combine with the water and 1/2 teaspoon salt in a saucepan and bring to a boil. Reduce the heat and cover the saucepan. Simmer for 45 minutes.

Combine the rice with the bread cubes, onion and sage in a large bowl. Season with 1/2 teaspoon salt and pepper to taste. Add the butter and pecans; toss to mix well. Spoon into a baking dish. Bake at 375 degrees for 30 to 45 minutes or until done to taste.

You may also spoon the stuffing into the cavity of and 8- to 10-pound turkey and roast using the directions with the turkey. A half-recipe will serve to stuff a 6- to 7-pound goose or roaster chicken.

*A*t *Central Market, everyone is a cook. When we were collecting recipes for this cookbook, we naturally turned to our store chefs, cooking instructors, customers and guest chefs. But we also got recipes and ideas from accounting, recruiting, bookkeeping, advertising and purchasing. Our customer correspondent, Carol, contributed the recipe for wild rice and fresh sage stuffing that does not need to be stuffed. In fact, we like it for lunch with a salad.*

Savory Biscotti

1/2 cup (1 stick) unsalted butter

2 1/2 cups flour

1 1/2 teaspoons baking powder

2 teaspoons kosher salt

1/4 teaspoon pepper

2 eggs

1/3 cup milk

3 tablespoons olive oil

1/4 cup drained capers

2 teaspoons grated lemon zest

1/4 cup finely chopped fresh flat-leaf parsley

1 egg

1 tablespoon water

pinch of salt

MAKES 4 DOZEN

Heat the butter in a small saucepan over medium heat for 5 to 7 minutes or until dark brown, taking care not to burn. Mix the flour, baking powder, kosher salt and pepper in a mixing bowl with a paddle attachment at low speed. Add the butter gradually and beat for 1 minute or until crumbly.

Whisk together 2 eggs, the milk and olive oil in a bowl. Add to the flour mixture and mix well. Stir in the capers, lemon zest and parsley.

Divide the dough into 4 portions. Shape into rolls 7 inches long on a lightly floured surface. Place on a baking sheet oiled with olive oil. Refrigerate, covered, for 30 minutes. Mix 1 egg, the water and a pinch of salt in a small bowl. Brush over the rolls.

Bake at 350 degrees for 30 to 40 minutes or until golden brown. Reduce the oven temperature to 250 degrees. Cool the rolls on a wire rack for 30 minutes. Slice the rolls diagonally 1/2 inch thick with a serrated knife. Arrange cut side down on a wire rack placed on a baking sheet.

Bake for 40 minutes or until crisp, turning over after 20 minutes. Cool completely on a wire rack. Store in an airtight container at room temperature for up to 1 week. Serve as an accompaniment to soups, stews and salads. Excellent with fresh goat cheese.

Provolone Crisps

1/2 cup (2 ounces) grated Romano cheese

1 1/2 cups (6 ounces) shredded provolone cheese

1/2 cup (1 stick) butter, softened

3 tablespoons water

2 drops of pepper sauce (optional)

1 cup flour

1 cup rolled oats or quick-cooking oats

1 teaspoon dried oregano leaves, crushed

1/2 teaspoon paprika

1/4 teaspoon salt

MAKES 3 TO 4 DOZEN

Reserve 1 tablespoon of the Romano cheese. Combine the remaining Romano cheese with the provolone cheese in a bowl. Add the butter, water and pepper sauce and mix well. Add the flour, oats, oregano, paprika and salt and mix to form a dough.

Shape the dough into a roll 1 1/2 to 2 inches in diameter. Wrap in plastic wrap and chill for 4 hours or longer. Cut the roll into 1/8-inch slices and sprinkle the slices with the reserved Romano cheese. Arrange on a buttered baking sheet.

Bake at 400 degrees for 10 minutes or until light brown. Remove to a wire rack to cool. Store in an airtight container for up to 1 week.

CM freshly baked breads make wonderful sandwiches. Try sardines and crisp bacon with mayonnaise on whole wheat toast; sliced roast lamb with mint jelly on Irish soda bread; tuna, chopped arugula and roasted red pepper on Parmesan bread; or sweet Gorgonzola cheese, sliced fresh figs and fresh mint on grilled challah bread.

Eggnog French Toast with Maple Syrup

4 cups eggnog

4 eggs

1 teaspoon freshly grated cinnamon

1/2 teaspoon freshly grated allspice

1 teaspoon freshly grated nutmeg

12 (1-inch) slices Central Market Challah Bread

1/4 cup (1/2 stick) unsalted butter

confectioners' sugar

maple syrup

SERVES 6

Whisk the eggnog, eggs, cinnamon, allspice and nutmeg together in a bowl. Arrange the bread slices in a single layer in a 10×15-inch baking pan. Pour the eggnog mixture over the bread slices. Chill, covered, for 2 to 3 hours. Let stand at room temperature for 20 minutes before cooking.

Heat 1 tablespoon of the butter in a heavy skillet over medium heat until melted and foamy.

Arrange as many bread slices as will fit in a single layer in the skillet. Cook until brown on both sides, turning once. Repeat with the remaining butter and bread slices.

Sprinkle the toast with confectioners' sugar and serve with maple syrup.

Although baking is an exact science, deciding how much to bake isn't. That's why we sometimes sell out of certain kinds of bread before the end of the day—and sometimes have some left over. Bread is definitely better the day it is baked, but sometimes you need to plan on having leftovers, for stuffing, bread puddings, bread crumbs, croutons and French toast.

To keep our bread fresh as long as possible, store it at room temperature in tightly sealed plastic bags. You can also freeze loaves for up to several months. Double-wrap them in plastic with as much air removed as possible, then wrap them in aluminum foil. With the bread still wrapped, thaw at room temperature.

Oatmeal Macadamia Pancakes

2 cups (or more) buttermilk

2 cups quick-cooking oats

2 eggs, beaten

1 tablespoon butter, melted and cooled

1/2 cup finely chopped macadamias

1/2 cup flour

2 tablespoons sugar

1 teaspoon baking powder

1 teaspoon baking soda

1/2 teaspoon cinnamon

pinch of salt

chopped macadamias

seasonal fruits

MAKES 1 DOZEN 4-INCH PANCAKES

Mix the buttermilk and oats in a medium bowl. Chill, covered, for 8 hours or longer. Add the eggs, butter and macadamias and mix well.

Sift the flour, sugar, baking powder, baking soda, cinnamon and salt together. Add to the oat mixture and whisk to form a thick batter, adding additional buttermilk if a thinner batter is preferred.

Heat a griddle or heavy skillet over medium heat until a drop of water will skate over the surface. Grease the griddle lightly. Ladle the batter by 1/4 cupfuls onto the griddle and cook for 2 minutes or until bubbles form on the surface; the edges should be dry and the bottoms golden brown. Turn the pancakes and cook for 1 minute on the other side. Sprinkle with chopped macadamias and seasonal fruits to serve.

$\mathcal{G}$ranita is the Italian word for "ice." For any combination, follow these basic instructions: Pour the mixture into a 9×13-inch metal pan and freeze for 45 minutes or until icy at the edges. Whisk to mix in the frozen portions. Freeze for 45 minutes or until slushy and icy at the edges and whisk again. Freeze for 3 hours or until solid. Scrape down the length of the pan with a fork to form ice flakes. Freeze for 1 hour to 1 week. Scoop into glasses, taking care not to smooth out the crystals.

Coffee Granita with Sambuca Cream

4 cups freshly brewed strong coffee

1 cup sugar

1 tablespoon grated orange zest

1 teaspoon vanilla extract

1 tablespoon sambuca or other anise-flavored liqueur

1 cup heavy whipping cream, whipped

sambuca to taste

SERVES 8

Combine the coffee, sugar, orange zest and vanilla in a bowl and mix to dissolve the sugar. Pour into a metal pan and chill for 2 hours. Stir in 1 tablespoon sambuca. Prepare using the instructions for Granitas on page 102. Spoon into goblets and top with whipped cream flavored with sambuca.

Watermelon Berry Granita

4 cups frozen Perfect Purée of Napa Valley Whata Watermelon, partially thawed

1/2 cup sugar

2 tablespoons fresh lemon juice

1 large strawberry

pinch of salt

SERVES 8

Process the watermelon purée, sugar, lemon juice, strawberry and salt in a blender until smooth. Prepare using the instructions for Granitas on page 102.

For **Papaya Granita,** substitute Perfect Purée of Napa Valley Hawaiian Style Papaya Purée for the watermelon purée and 1 cup of water for the lemon juice in this recipe.

Basic Smoothie

8 ounces fruit juice

1 banana

12 ounces frozen fruit

SERVES 2

Combine the ingredients in a blender in the order of softest to hardest, in this case, the fruit juice, banana and frozen fruit, blending at low speed for 30 seconds. Increase the speed to high and process until smooth.

You should turn the blender off, shake the contents to the side of the blender and blend again if any frozen fruit jams the blender. You may also add additional juice and shake the fruit to the side to allow the liquid to reach the bottom of the blender and then blend again.

CM suggests the following variations on the Basic Smoothie: Add additional frozen fruit for a thicker smoothie. Omit the banana and increase the fruit juice to 12 ounces. Substitute 4 ounces of yogurt or soft tofu for 4 ounces of the fruit juice.

Reduce sweetness and calories by substituting 4 ounces of water for 4 ounces of the fruit juice and/or 6 ounces of ice for 6 ounces of the frozen fruit. Improve nutritional content with wheat germ, protein powder, flax oil, spirulina, fiber or other supplements.

More Smoothies

Tsunami Smoothie

Combine 4 ounces CM apple lemon ginger juice, 4 ounces pineapple juice, 1 banana, 6 ounces frozen mango and 6 ounces frozen papaya in the order listed using the instructions in the Basic Smoothie recipe on page 104.

Piña Colada Smoothie

Combine 8 ounces pineapple-coconut juice, 1 teaspoon shredded coconut, 1 banana, 8 ounces frozen pineapple and 4 ounces ice in the order listed using the instructions in the Basic Smoothie recipe on page 104.

Platanade Smoothie

Combine 4 ounces milk, 1 teaspoon honey, $1/8$ teaspoon cinnamon, $1/8$ teaspoon nutmeg, 2 bananas and 8 to 10 ounces ice in the order listed using the instructions in the Basic Smoothie recipe on page 104.

Peanut Butter Banana Smoothie

Combine 4 ounces skim milk or soy milk, 1 tablespoon peanut butter, 1 teaspoon honey, 2 tablespoons protein powder, 2 bananas and 6 ounces ice in the order listed using the instructions in the Basic Smoothie recipe on page 104.

Amber Tea Delight

8 teaspoons instant tea

2 cups cold water

3¹/2 cups apricot nectar

2 cups orange juice

¹/2 cup lemon juice

¹/2 cup sugar

1¹/2 quarts ginger ale, chilled

SERVES 15 TO 18

Dissolve the instant tea in the cold water in a pitcher. Add the apricot nectar, orange juice, lemon juice and sugar and mix well. Chill until serving time. Add the ginger ale just before serving. Serve over ice in tall glasses.

Strawberry Iced Tea

¹/3 cup sugar

1 cup water

4 cups freshly brewed tea

1 cup Central Market strawberry apple juice

4 whole strawberries

SERVES 4

Mix the sugar and water in a saucepan. Bring to a boil and cook until the sugar dissolves, stirring occasionally. Let stand until cool.

Add the brewed tea and strawberry apple juice and mix well. Pour over ice in tall glasses and garnish each glass with a strawberry.

Tropical Sparkling Sangria

1 bottle of Spanish white wine, chilled

1 mango, cut into 1/2-inch pieces

12 ounces Looza mango nectar, chilled

2 limes, thinly sliced

2 small carambolas (star fruit), thinly sliced crosswise, or 1/2 cup golden pineapple chunks

12 ounces ginger ale, chilled

1 bottle of sparkling Spanish Cava, chilled

MAKES 2 1/2 QUARTS

Combine the white wine, mango, mango nectar, limes and carambolas in a large pitcher and mix well. Chill until serving time or for up to 1 day.

Add the ginger ale, sparkling wine and ice cubes at serving time. Pour into glasses to serve and garnish with the lime and carambola slices.

Classic Sangria

1 1/2 ounces brandy

1 quart (4 cups) orange juice

1 quart (4 cups) pineapple juice

1 bottle of hearty Spanish red wine

1/2 cup sugar

SERVES 10

Combine the brandy, orange juice, pineapple juice, wine and sugar in a large pitcher and mix to dissolve the sugar. Chill for 2 hours. Pour into glasses and add sliced fruit, such as oranges, limes, strawberries and peaches.

DESSERTS

Treats make us sweeter. A great dessert makes dinner
into a celebration. Whether it's the reward for the backyard chore
of churning ice cream or the crowning finish to a
five-course meal, dessert is a culmination, a high point.
That doesn't mean it has to be complicated, difficult or tricky.
A dessert is only required to delight. At Central Market,
we try to make sure there's a surprise around every corner.
We love to hear the "oohs" and "aahs" when a customer
first tastes a sample of Miles of Chocolate or a child
takes a bite out of a macaroon.
"Ooh" and "aah"—that's the sound of dessert. Try these.

Hazelnut Shortcakes with Fresh Berries and Ginger Cream

Shortcakes

3/4 cup hazelnuts, toasted, skinned and cooled

1/3 cup sugar

2 cups flour

1 tablespoon baking powder

1/2 teaspoon salt

1/2 cup (1 stick) unsalted butter, chilled and cut into pieces

1/2 cup plus 2 tablespoons heavy cream

1 teaspoon sugar

Ginger Cream

1 1/2 cups heavy cream

1 tablespoon sugar

1 teaspoon minced candied ginger

Berries

1 pint raspberries

1 pint strawberries, cut into quarters

1 pint blackberries

1 pint blueberries

1 teaspoon grated orange zest

1 to 2 tablespoons sugar

SERVES 6

For the shortcakes, grind the hazelnuts with 1/3 cup sugar in a food processor. Combine with the flour, baking powder and salt in a bowl. Cut in the butter until the mixture is crumbly. Add 1/2 cup plus 1 tablespoon of the cream gradually, mixing with a fork just until the dough forms a ball.

Pat the dough into a circle 1 inch thick on a lightly floured surface. Cut into six 2 1/2-inch circles and arrange on a baking sheet. Brush with the remaining 1 tablespoon cream and sprinkle with 1 teaspoon sugar. Bake at 350 degrees for 30 minutes or until golden brown. Let stand until slightly cooled.

For the ginger cream, beat the whipping cream with the sugar and ginger at high speed in a mixing bowl until soft peaks form.

For the berries, combine the raspberries, strawberries, blackberries, blueberries, orange zest and sugar in a bowl. Toss gently to mix.

To assemble, cut the shortcakes into halves horizontally and place the bottom halves on serving plates. Spoon half the berries on the shortcake bottoms and pipe the ginger cream over the berries. Spoon the remaining berries over the ginger cream and top with the shortcake tops. Serve immediately.

Irish Cream Banana Pudding

1 (16-ounce) package rectangular butter cookies

8 medium bananas, thinly sliced

1 (5-ounce) package vanilla instant pudding mix

2 cups milk

1 teaspoon ground cinnamon

1/4 teaspoon freshly grated nutmeg

pinch of salt

8 ounces Neufchâtel cheese, softened

1 (14-ounce) can sweetened condensed milk

1 tablespoon Irish cream liqueur

1 tablespoon vanilla extract

1 1/2 cups whipping cream

1/4 cup sugar

1 teaspoon vanilla extract

SERVES 8 TO 10

Line the bottom of a 9×13-inch dish with a single layer of butter cookies, using any broken cookies for this layer. Add an even layer of the sliced bananas.

Combine the pudding mix, milk, cinnamon, nutmeg and salt in a medium bowl and beat until the mixture thickens. Beat the Neufchâtel cheese in a mixing bowl until light. Beat in the sweetened condensed milk, liqueur and 1 tablespoon vanilla. Fold in the pudding mixture.

Beat the whipping cream with the sugar and 1 teaspoon vanilla in a mixing bowl. Fold gently into the pudding mixture. Spread over the sliced bananas and smooth with the back of the spoon. Top with a single layer of the remaining cookies. Cover with plastic wrap and chill for 2 hours or longer before serving.

You may substitute whipped topping for the whipped cream mixture if preferred.

Dried Cherry and Hazelnut Bread Pudding

Pudding

4 cups day-old Central Market
bread, such as cinnamon rolls,
croissants or French bread

1/3 cup dried cherries

1/3 cup toasted hazelnuts

4 eggs

2 1/4 cups half-and-half

3/4 cup sugar

1 tablespoon vanilla extract

Rum Sauce

1/2 cup (1 stick) unsalted butter

1 cup sugar

2 egg yolks

1/4 cup water

1/4 cup dark rum

SERVES 6

For the pudding, sprinkle half the bread cubes in 6 large ramekins sprayed with nonstick cooking spray. Sprinkle the cherries, half the hazelnuts, the remaining bread and the remaining hazelnuts into the ramekins.

Beat the eggs in a bowl. Add the half-and-half, sugar and vanilla and beat until smooth. Pour over the layers in the ramekins, pressing down to distribute evenly. Arrange the ramekins in a 9×13-inch baking pan.

Place the baking pan in a 350-degree oven and pour in enough boiling water to measure 1 inch. Bake for 35 to 45 minutes or until a knife inserted near the center comes out clean.

For the sauce, combine the butter, sugar, egg yolks and water in a saucepan. Cook over medium heat until the sugar melts and the mixture begins to bubble, whisking constantly. Remove from the heat and stir in the rum. Cool slightly and serve with the warm pudding.

Stilton Cheesecake

1¹/4 cups flour

¹/4 cup sugar

7 tablespoons butter, softened

8 ounces Stilton cheese, trimmed and crumbled

24 ounces cream cheese, softened

1 cup sugar

¹/3 cup flour

3 eggs

8 ounces (1 cup) sour cream

2 teaspoons vanilla extract

SERVES 8

Combine the flour, sugar and butter in a food processor and process to form coarse crumbs. Press evenly over the bottom of a buttered 8- or 9-inch springform pan. Bake at 350 degrees for 20 to 30 minutes or until light brown. Cool to room temperature. Reduce the oven temperature to 300 degrees.

Combine the Stilton cheese, cream cheese and sugar in a large mixing bowl and beat until smooth. Beat in the flour. Add the eggs 1 at a time, mixing well after each addition. Beat in the sour cream and vanilla.

Spoon over the prepared crust. Bake for 1¹/2 hours or until set and golden brown. Cool to room temperature. Chill in the refrigerator. Place on a serving plate and remove the side of the springform pan.

Serve with fresh fruit, Key Lime or Lemon Curd, Fig & Walnut Sauce or Saba syrup, all of which can be found at Central Market.

How passionate are we about food? Real passionate. We cater a lot of weddings and design flowers for even more, but in 1995, Central Market actually hosted a wedding—in the store. The sentimental couple decided to tie the knot in the place they first met, which happened to be in the cheese department of the North Lamar store in Austin.

On a busy Saturday, violinists played classical music while the bride and groom exchanged vows over the Parmigiano-Reggiano. The bakery supplied a (cheese) cake, and dewy-eyed customers stopped their carts to join guests in a toast to the happy couple and throw rice (arborio, of course).

Orange Dream Cheesecake

Cookie Crumb Crust

1 1/3 cups crushed sugar cookies or pecan sandies

1 tablespoon sugar

1/4 cup (1/2 stick) butter

Filling

1 egg white

16 ounces cream cheese, softened

3 eggs

1 egg yolk

1/2 cup (1 stick) butter, softened

1 cup sugar

1 tablespoon cornstarch

1 teaspoon baking powder

1/3 cup frozen orange juice concentrate, thawed

Orange Topping

1 1/4 cups sour cream

2 1/2 tablespoons sugar

1 teaspoon frozen orange juice concentrate, thawed

SERVES 8 TO 10

For the crust, combine the cookie crumbs, sugar and butter in a bowl and mix well. Press into a buttered 9-inch springform pan. Bake at 325 degrees for 10 minutes. Cool slightly.

For the filling, beat the egg white in a small bowl until stiff peaks form. Combine the cream cheese, eggs, egg yolk and butter in a large mixing bowl and beat at medium speed until light and fluffy. Add the sugar, cornstarch, baking powder and orange juice concentrate and beat for 2 minutes. Fold in the beaten egg white.

Spoon into the prepared crust. Bake at 325 degrees for 1 hour. Turn off the oven and let the cheesecake stand in the oven for 30 minutes longer.

For the topping, combine the sour cream, sugar and orange juice concentrate in a bowl and mix well. Spread over the cheesecake. Let stand until cool.

Chill the cheesecake for 3 hours or longer. Place on a serving plate and remove the side of the springform pan.

Basic Fresh Fruit Sorbet

1/2 cup sugar

1 cup water

2 tablespoons corn syrup

2 teaspoons lemon juice

2 cups fresh fruit purée

SERVES 4 TO 6

Bring the sugar and water to a boil in a small saucepan. Remove from the heat and stir to dissolve the sugar. Stir in the corn syrup. Cool to room temperature.

Add the lemon juice and fruit purée and mix well. Adjust the sugar if necessary for taste. Chill until very cold.

Freeze in an ice cream freezer using the manufacturer's directions.

Many fruits can be used for sorbets, including kiwifruit, mangoes, papayas and berries. You should, however, strain the purée of raspberries, blueberries and blackberries.

To use lemons and limes, use 2 cups of the juice with 1 teaspoon of the grated zest and increase the sugar to 1 cup.

To use oranges, use 2 cups of the juice with 1 teaspoon of the grated zest, but no additional sugar. Mixtures of fruits and herbs make for interesting flavor combinations.

Herbs that can be used to flavor sorbets include cinnamon, fennel, ginger, lemon grass, lemon verbena, mint, tarragon, thyme and even black pepper. Herbs should be infused in the hot sugar syrup, cooled and strained for the best results.

Wines such as Champagne and Merlot make delicious sorbets for cleansing the palate.

Mint-to-Be Ice Cream

10 Oreo cookies

$1/3$ cup Starlight
peppermint candies

2 ounces semisweet chocolate,
at room temperature

5 eggs

$1^1/2$ cups sugar

4 cups heavy cream

2 cups 2% milk

$1^1/2$ tablespoons peppermint
extract

red food coloring

SERVES 8

Cut the cookies into quarters. Crush the mints into small pieces. Shave the chocolate with a straight-edge knife or cleaver. Place the cookies, mints and chocolates in the freezer and freeze until firm.

Whisk the eggs in a bowl for 1 minute or until light. Whisk in the sugar gradually until smooth. Whisk in the cream, milk and peppermint extract.

Stir in enough food coloring to color the mixture pale pink.

Pour into the container of an ice cream freezer and freeze using the manufacturer's directions. Remove the paddle from the container and stir in the frozen cookies, mints and chocolate. Store in the freezer until very firm.

Every time we open a new store, we suffer a little parental anxiety, wondering whether any customers will show up. In Fort Worth, in October of 2001, there was special cause for concern because it was our first foray into North Texas. We shouldn't have worried.

On that warm Wednesday, the crowd started forming a couple of hours before the door opened for the first time, and a line of people extended halfway around the side of the building for most of the day. As our new customers waited to get inside, we served them cold bottled water and samples of our freshly squeezed juices.

The lively beauty of fresh seasonal fruit often eclipses the appeal of its drabber, chewier, dried cousin. But shelf life is not the only advantage of dried fruit—really, it is a delicacy unto itself, and there are more varieties available than ever in Central Market's Bulk Foods department.

Dried fruit has much more sweetness and flavor than regular fruit—lots more intensity (not to mention calories by weight, because all the water has been removed). Keep several kinds on hand for using in baked goods or compotes, and don't forget that dried fruits are excellent on a cheese plate with nuts and soft, fruity wines.

Tippie Creek Fruit Cobbler

1/2 cup (1 stick) butter

2 cups flour

2 cups sugar

4 teaspoons baking powder

1 1/2 cups milk

1 pound fresh peaches, sliced, or frozen sliced peaches

SERVES 6 TO 8

Place the butter in a 9×13-inch baking dish. Place in a 350-degree oven for 5 minutes or until melted; spread evenly.

Combine the flour, sugar, baking powder and milk in a bowl and mix until smooth. Spoon into the prepared dish. Spread the fruit over the batter.

Place on the center oven rack and bake at 350 degrees for 45 minutes to 1 hour. Serve warm with ice cream or whipped cream.

You may substitute fresh or frozen berries for the peaches.

Armagnac Plum Tart

Almond Crust

$1/4$ cup sliced almonds

2 teaspoons sugar

1 cup flour

$1/2$ teaspoon salt

$1/2$ cup (1 stick) butter, chilled or frozen, cut into chunks

$1^1/2$ tablespoons ice water

Filling

3 eggs

1 cup heavy cream

1 tablespoon Armagnac

$1/2$ cup confectioners' sugar

$1/2$ teaspoon almond extract or vanilla extract

8 to 12 large fresh plums, cut into halves

SERVES 8

For the crust, combine the almonds and sugar in a food processor and process until finely ground. Add the flour and salt and pulse to mix. Add the butter and process to fine crumbs. Add the ice water and process until the mixture forms a ball.

Roll the dough into a circle on a lightly floured surface. Fit into a fluted tart pan with a detachable side. Place in the freezer to chill.

For the filling, beat the eggs in a medium mixing bowl until light yellow. Add the cream, Armagnac, confectioners' sugar and almond extract; mix until smooth. Arrange the plum halves cut side down in concentric circles in the tart pan and pour the cream mixture over the top.

Bake at 425 degrees for 20 minutes. Reduce the oven temperature to 375 degrees and bake for 30 minutes or until the filling is set and the crust is golden brown.

Cool the tart on a wire rack. Place on a serving plate and remove the side of the pan.

Eiswein Truffles

6 ounces bittersweet chocolate

1/2 cup heavy cream

2 tablespoons Eiswein

1/2 cup unsweetened baking cocoa, sifted confectioners' sugar or finely ground toasted skinless hazelnuts

MAKES 18

Chop the chocolate very fine and place in a metal bowl. Bring the cream just to a boil in a saucepan and pour over the chocolate, stirring until the chocolate melts completely. Stir in the wine. Place plastic wrap directly on the surface of the chocolate mixture. Chill for 2 hours or until very firm.

Scoop the chocolate into small balls with a melon baller and place on a tray lined with foil. Freeze for 10 minutes. Roll the balls lightly between the hands for several seconds if the surface appears dry after freezing. Roll the balls in baking cocoa, confectioners' sugar or finely ground hazelnuts. Place in small paper candy cups to serve.

Store the truffles in an airtight container in the refrigerator for up to 1 week or in the freezer for up to 1 month.

You may scoop the chilled mixture by rounded teaspoonfuls into 1-inch mounds on the foil-lined tray or roll into balls with hands dusted with baking cocoa or confectioners' sugar if preferred. You may also substitute any flavored liqueur for the Eiswein.

CM stocks Eiswein, a unique sweet dessert wine produced in Germany in one of the coldest wine regions in the world. In fact, the grapes are picked when frozen on the vine, producing a wine that is exceptionally sweet but with balanced acidity.

Chocolate Mayonnaise Cake with Chocolate Drizzle Icing

Cake

4 cups flour

2 cups sugar

$1/2$ cup plus 2 tablespoons baking cocoa

4 teaspoons baking soda

$1/2$ teaspoon salt

2 cups mayonnaise

2 cups water

2 teaspoons vanilla extract

Chocolate Drizzle Icing

3 ounces unsweetened chocolate

2 cups sugar

$2/3$ cup milk

6 tablespoons ($3/4$ stick) butter

$1/2$ teaspoon salt

1 teaspoon vanilla extract

1 cup chopped pecans

SERVES 16

For the cake, mix the flour, sugar, baking cocoa, baking soda and salt in a large mixing bowl. Add the mayonnaise, water and vanilla and beat until smooth. Spread in a heavily buttered and floured bundt pan.

Place the bundt pan on the center rack in an oven heated to 350 degrees. Bake for 50 to 60 minutes or until a wooden pick inserted in the center comes out clean. Cool in the pan on a wire rack for 30 minutes. Invert onto a cake plate to cool completely.

For the icing, combine the chocolate, sugar, milk, butter and salt in a small saucepan. Bring to a boil over medium-low heat, stirring constantly. Boil briskly for 1 minute. Remove from the heat and stir in the vanilla. Cool to lukewarm and fold in the pecans. Drizzle over the cooled cake. You may sprinkle with the pecans if preferred.

123

Chocolate Cakes with Melted Caramel Centers

1 1/4 cups (2 1/2 sticks) butter

4 ounces semisweet chocolate, chopped

1/2 cup sugar

3/4 cup flour

3 tablespoons baking cocoa

1 teaspoon baking powder

3 eggs

1 egg yolk

6 caramel candies, unwrapped and cut into halves

1/2 cup prepared hot fudge sauce

1/2 cup prepared caramel sauce

SERVES 6

Heat the butter in a medium saucepan until melted and bubbling but not brown. Remove from the heat and stir in the chocolate and sugar. Let stand for 5 minutes. Pour into a large bowl and beat until smooth.

Sift the flour, baking cocoa and baking powder together. Add to the chocolate mixture 1/3 at a time, mixing well and scraping the bowl after each addition. Beat in the eggs and egg yolk 1 at a time. Beat at high speed for 10 minutes.

Spoon the batter into six 8-ounce ramekins sprayed with nonstick cooking spray, filling the ramekins halfway. Place 2 caramel halves in the center of each ramekin. Fill the ramekins with the remaining batter. Place the ramekins on a baking sheet.

Place the baking sheet on the center rack of an oven heated to 350 degrees. Bake for 16 to 18 minutes or until the edges are set but the center is still soft.

Warm the chocolate sauce and caramel sauce in separate small saucepans. Remove the cakes from the oven and loosen from the sides of the ramekins with a thin sharp knife. Drizzle the warmed sauces onto dessert plates and invert the cakes onto the plates. Serve immediately.

Blueberry Pound Cake

Cake

3 cups flour

2 cups fresh blueberries

1 teaspoon baking powder

1/2 teaspoon baking soda

1/2 cup (1 stick) margarine, softened

4 ounces cream cheese, softened

2 cups sugar

3 eggs

1 egg white

8 ounces (1 cup) lemon yogurt

2 teaspoons vanilla extract

Lemon Glaze

1 cup confectioners' sugar

1 tablespoon lemon juice

1 tablespoon hot water

SERVES 16

For the cake, toss 2 tablespoons of the flour with the blueberries in a small bowl to coat evenly. Mix the remaining flour with the baking powder and baking soda.

Cream the margarine, cream cheese and sugar in a mixing bowl, beating at medium speed for 5 minutes or until light and fluffy. Beat in the eggs and egg white 1 at a time, mixing well after each addition. Add the flour mixture alternately with the yogurt, beginning and ending with the flour mixture and mixing well after each addition. Fold in the blueberries and vanilla.

Spoon into a 10-inch tube pan coated with nonstick cooking spray. Bake at 350 degrees for 1 hour and 10 minutes or until a wooden pick inserted in the center comes out clean. Cool in the pan on a wire rack for 1 hour. Remove to a cake plate.

For the glaze, combine the confectioners' sugar, lemon juice and hot water in a small bowl and mix until smooth. Drizzle over the warm cake. Cut the cake with a serrated knife to serve.

Colonial Inn Cake

1 cup flour

2 teaspoons baking powder

1/2 teaspoon salt

4 egg whites

1/2 cup sugar

4 egg yolks

1/2 cup sugar

1/4 cup water

1 teaspoon vanilla extract

1/4 cup sliced almonds

1 tablespoon sugar

1 (31/4-ounce) package vanilla pudding mix

1 cup heavy whipping cream, chilled

sugar to taste

SERVES 16

Sift the flour, baking powder and salt together. Beat the egg whites in a small mixing bowl until foamy. Add 1/2 cup sugar gradually, beating until stiff and glossy.

Beat the egg yolks in a large mixing bowl until light yellow. Add 1/2 cup sugar, the water and the vanilla gradually, beating until smooth. Add the sifted dry ingredients and beat at low speed for 30 seconds. Increase the speed to high and beat for 2 minutes longer. Fold in the egg whites gently.

Spread the batter in 2 greased and floured round 9-inch cake pans. Mix the almonds and 1 tablespoon sugar in a small bowl and sprinkle over the top of 1 layer. Bake at 325 degrees for 30 minutes. Cool in the pans for 10 minutes and remove to a wire rack to cool completely.

Prepare the pudding mix using the package directions. Beat the whipping cream with enough sugar to sweeten in a bowl until soft peaks form. Split the cooled cake layers into halves horizontally. Reserve the almond layer and place 1 of the other layers on a cake plate. Spread with half the pudding and top with a second layer. Spread with the whipped cream and top with a third layer. Spread with the remaining pudding and top with the almond layer. Store in the refrigerator.

Best-Ever Cookies

3^1/2 cups flour

1 teaspoon salt

1 cup (2 sticks) butter, softened

1 cup sugar

1 cup packed light brown sugar

1 egg

1 cup vegetable oil

1 cup crushed cornflakes

1 cup rolled oats

^{1}/2 cup shredded coconut

1^1/2 cups chopped pecans

2 teaspoons vanilla extract

MAKES 5 TO 7 DOZEN

Sift the flour and salt together. Cream the butter with the sugar and brown sugar in a mixing bowl until light and fluffy. Beat in the egg, then the oil. Add the cornflakes, oats, coconut and pecans in the order listed and mix well after each addition. Add the flour mixture and mix well. Stir in the vanilla.

Shape into walnut-size balls and place on an ungreased cookie sheet; press with a fork to flatten. Bake at 325 degrees for 14 minutes or just until golden brown; do not overbake. Cool the cookies on the cookie sheet for 5 minutes and remove to a wire rack to cool completely.

Outrageous Chocolate Chip Cookies

2¹/2 cups sifted flour

1 teaspoon baking soda

1 teaspoon salt

1 cup (2 sticks) unsalted butter, softened

³/4 cup sugar

³/4 cup packed light brown sugar

2 teaspoons Madagascar vanilla extract

2 eggs, at room temperature

1 (12-ounce) package semisweet or double chocolate chips, or a mixture

¹/2 to 1 (11-ounce) package white chocolate chips

¹/2 (11-ounce) package toffee chips

¹/2 to 1 cup chopped pecans or walnuts (optional)

MAKES 3 DOZEN

Mix the flour, baking soda and salt together. Cream the butter, sugar, brown sugar and vanilla in a large mixing bowl until light and fluffy. Add the eggs and mix well. Add the dry ingredients gradually, mixing well after each addition. Stir in the chocolate chips, white chocolate chips, toffee chips and pecans.

Drop by rounded tablespoonfuls onto an ungreased cookie sheet. Bake at 350 degrees for 12 to 13 minutes for chewy cookies or for 13 to 15 minutes for crisp cookies. Cool on the cookie sheet for 5 minutes and remove to a wire rack to cool completely.

Our scan manager (whatever that is), Kathy, tinkered with the classic chocolate chip cookie to come up with this totally outrageous version. "I'd been making chocolate chip cookies for years for my kids," she says. "After working at Central Market, I just got to thinking, what if I made them with REAL vanilla and REAL chocolate chips—Ghirardelli chips and Madagascar vanilla."

CM Coconut Macaroons

5¹/4 cups unsweetened dried shredded coconut

3 tablespoons pastry flour

1 cup egg whites, about 8 eggs

1¹/2 teaspoons vanilla extract

pinch of salt

1 cup sugar

3 tablespoons white corn syrup

¹/4 cup water

MAKES 16 LARGE OR 32 SMALL MACAROONS

Combine the coconut, pastry flour, egg whites, vanilla and salt in a mixing bowl and mix at the lowest speed. Blend the sugar and corn syrup in a small saucepan and stir in the water. Cook until the sugar dissolves, stirring constantly. Bring just to the boiling point without stirring and remove from the heat. Drizzle into the coconut mixture very gradually, beating constantly at the lowest speed. Beat until the mixture is just warm.

Line a baking sheet with baking parchment or spray with nonstick cooking spray. Pipe the coconut mixture onto the baking sheet with a pastry bag fitted with a large cone tip or scoop onto the baking sheet. Bake at 350 degrees for 10 to 12 minutes or until the tops are golden brown. Cool on the baking sheet for 5 minutes and remove to a wire rack to cool completely.

CM carries the unsweetened dried shredded coconut and the pastry flour used in this recipe in the Bulk department.

CM Cowboy Cookies

2 cups flour

1/2 teaspoon baking powder

1 teaspoon baking soda

1 cup sugar

1 cup packed brown sugar

1/2 teaspoon salt

2 eggs

2 cups rolled oats

2 teaspoons vanilla extract

1 cup Valrhona milk chocolate disks

11/2 cups Valrhona dark chocolate disks

1 cup (2 sticks) butter, melted

MAKES 7 DOZEN

Mix the flour, baking powder, baking soda, sugar, brown sugar and salt in a large bowl. Add the eggs, oats, vanilla, milk chocolate and dark chocolate. Pour the butter over the ingredients and mix well.

Drop by teaspoonfuls 2 inches apart onto a lightly greased cookie sheet. Bake at 350 degrees for 15 minutes or until golden brown. Cool on the cookie sheet for 5 minutes and remove to a wire rack to cool completely.

SIGNATURE EVENTS

Grilling
Hatch Festival
Mardi Gras
Holiday

Over the last ten years, we've created many ways to share

our knowledge and enthusiasm for the limitless possibilities of food.

We've honored Texas Independence Day, and while the adults were learning

how to prepare wild Texas game, the kids were learning how to

rope a calf. We've made it snow in July, explored the world of chocolate,

gone crazy with Tomatomania and come to our senses again

with Living Well, our ode to health and well-being.

The Austin store has hosted the Italian Chalk Art Festival and Plano

has launched hot air balloons. And one recent day saw a tuba band

in the parking lot of the San Antonio store. (Who knew there were

bands of tubas? We always thought one was enough.)

These seasonally inspired occasions come and go depending on mood

and opportunity, but certain celebrations are especially memorable.

You'll recognize them: Summer's salute to Hatch chiles, Mardi Gras,

our kick-off to the Grilling season and the Holiday Open House.

We hope the next few pages will remind you of those glorious seasons

past and inspire many special gatherings to come.

Grilling is a transformative process. Even more than other cooking methods, the smoke and char imparted by live coals gives foods a whole new flavor profile, demanding different wines and more vivid side dishes. We know it works wonders on food, but we think grilling also has a magic effect on a gathering. We grill everything at Central Market— seafood, meats, sausages, chicken, even vegetables, fruits and salads.

At the 2003 Saveur Texas Hill Country Wine and Food Festival, we even grilled pizza (see page 142). To say that was a hit is a classic understatement. People were grabbing pizza right off the grill, stampeding over a low fence that strained to separate them from our cooking staff.

Grilled Hamburgers with Cognac, Mustard and Chives

1¹/2 pounds ground beef

1¹/2 tablespoons Cognac

2 teaspoons Dijon mustard

1 tablespoon minced fresh chives

1 teaspoon salt

¹/2 teaspoon freshly ground pepper

5 Central Market Whole Wheat Buns

5 large tomato slices

sunflower sprouts

SERVES 5

Combine the ground beef with the Cognac, Dijon mustard, chives, salt and pepper in a bowl and mix well. Shape into 5 large patties.

Grill the patties over medium-hot coals for 7 to 10 minutes on each side or until done to taste. Serve on the buns with the tomato slices and sunflower sprouts.

Roquefort Flank Steak

1/2 cup (2 ounces) crumbled Roquefort cheese
1/4 cup thinly sliced green onions with tops
2 garlic cloves, minced
1/4 teaspoon hot pepper sauce
1/4 teaspoon pepper
1 (1 1/2-pound) beef flank steak, at room temperature

SERVES 4 TO 6

Combine the Roquefort cheese, green onions, garlic, pepper sauce and pepper in a bowl and mix well.

Grill the steak over medium-hot coals for 10 to 15 minutes for medium-rare or until done to taste, turning once and spooning the sauce over the steak during the last 5 minutes of grilling time.

Remove the steak to a cutting board and let stand for 5 minutes. Slice diagonally across the grain to serve.

Try some of these marinade ideas:

All-purpose—lemon juice, black pepper, garlic, chopped fresh herbs, olive oil

Pork—soy sauce, mirin, cider vinegar, sugar, ginger, beer

Chicken—olive oil, garlic, cilantro, mint, curry powder

Chicken or pork—garlic, onion, orange and lime juice, ground cumin, oregano, cilantro, olive oil

Chicken, shrimp or pork—vegetable oil, toasted sesame oil, soy sauce, garlic, ginger, chopped scallions

Beef—tequila, soy sauce, lime juice, cilantro, garlic, cumin, oregano, olive oil

Fish—lemon juice, olive oil, garlic, shallot, anchovy paste, capers, pepper

Central Market takes a lot of pride in cooking good food, but we don't have an attitude about it. So, along with exotic ways to prepare baby lamb and wild lettuces, this cookbook calls for ingredients that some gourmets might eschew—pantry items like packaged seasoning blends and biscuit mix, bottled sauces and beer. It's all about playing with food.

The marinade used with these ribs is a favorite with some loyal customers, and it just goes to show that you don't need to do much to make a meal special. Just let your imagination run wild in a well-stocked kitchen.

Ravishing Ribs

1 1/2 cups Steen's Pure Cane Syrup

1/2 cup soy sauce

6 pounds pork spareribs or baby back ribs

Beau Monde seasoning

SERVES 4 TO 6

Mix the syrup and soy sauce together in a bowl. Cut the ribs into 3- or 4-rib sections. Rub generously with Beau Monde seasoning. Place in a shallow dish. Brush generously with the syrup mixture. Marinate for 1 hour.

Drain the ribs, reserving the marinade. Place the ribs bone side down on a grill over low coals. Grill for 45 to 50 minutes or until cooked through, brushing frequently with the reserved marinade.

You may also grill the ribs using an indirect heat method. Sear the ribs over the coals and then move them to a section of the grill away from the coals and grill with the cover closed. You may substitute chicken for the ribs, using the same marinade, if preferred.

You may use the marinade for many purposes, increasing the amounts as needed in a 3 to 1 ratio.

Asian Marinated Grilled Tuna

4 (8-ounce) yellowfin tuna steaks

1 (10-ounce) bottle of teriyaki sauce

1/3 cup dry sherry

3 tablespoons chopped gingerroot

1/3 cup chopped scallions

2 or 3 garlic cloves, sliced

juice of 2 lemons

3 tablespoons rice wine vinegar

2 teaspoons freshly ground pepper

2 tablespoons olive oil

SERVES 4

Arrange the tuna steaks in a single layer in a shallow dish. Combine the teriyaki sauce, sherry, gingerroot, chopped scallions, garlic, lemon juice, vinegar and pepper in a bowl and mix well. Pour over the tuna. Marinate, covered, in the refrigerator for 2 hours, turning the tuna once.

Drain the tuna and allow to come to room temperature. Rub on all sides with the olive oil. Place at a 45-degree angle to the grill rack over hot coals. Grill for 1 minute. Turn the steaks 90 degrees on the rack to create a crosshatch grill mark. Grill for 1 minute longer. Turn the steaks over and repeat the process; the tuna will be rare and cool in the center. Cook for 2 minutes longer on each side for medium. Serve with pickled ginger and sliced scallion greens.

Tandoori Chicken Sandwiches

Spicy Tandoori Sauce

1 cup packed fresh mint leaves

1 cup packed fresh cilantro leaves

1 jalapeño chile, seeded and minced

3 tablespoons chopped onion

2 teaspoons apple cider vinegar

1/2 cup mayonnaise

salt and pepper to taste

Sandwiches

6 boneless skinless chicken breasts

2 tablespoons fresh lemon juice

1 cup plain yogurt

1 1/2 tablespoons chopped gingerroot

2 garlic cloves, minced

1/2 teaspoon cumin

1/2 teaspoon coriander

1/4 teaspoon turmeric

1/4 teaspoon cayenne pepper

6 rounds naan bread

SERVES 6

For the sauce, combine the mint, cilantro, chile and onion in a food processor and pulse until finely chopped. Add the vinegar and mayonnaise and process just until combined. Season with salt and pepper. Spoon into a covered container and chill until serving time or for up to 3 days.

For the sandwiches, arrange the chicken in a single layer in a shallow dish. Sprinkle with the lemon juice. Mix the yogurt with the gingerroot, garlic, cumin, coriander, turmeric and cayenne pepper in a bowl. Spoon over the chicken, turning to coat well. Marinate, covered, in the refrigerator for 4 to 6 hours; drain.

Grill the chicken over medium-high heat for 5 minutes. Turn and grill for 5 minutes longer or until cooked through. Let stand until slightly cooled.

Toast the bread rounds lightly on the grill. Cut each round into halves horizontally. Spread the cut sides of each round with the sauce.

Slice the chicken diagonally and arrange the slices over half the rounds; top with the remaining halves. Cut each sandwich into halves and serve warm or at room temperature.

Grilled Chicken Breasts with
Papaya, Cucumber and Tomato Salsa

Papaya, Cucumber and Tomato Salsa

1 papaya, peeled and seeded

1 cucumber, peeled and seeded

1 medium tomato, seeded

1/4 to 1 teaspoon minced
jalapeño chile

1 teaspoon thinly sliced
fresh chives

1 teaspoon chopped
fresh cilantro

1 teaspoon sugar

1 tablespoon vegetable oil

1 tablespoon seasoned rice
wine vinegar

1/2 teaspoon kosher salt

Chicken

1 tablespoon olive oil

1 teaspoon minced garlic

1 tablespoon chili powder

1/2 teaspoon oregano

1/4 teaspoon cumin

1/2 teaspoon kosher salt

6 boneless skinless
chicken breasts

SERVES 6

For the salsa, cut the papaya, cucumber and tomato into 1/4-inch pieces. Combine with the chile, chives and cilantro in a bowl. Add the sugar, oil, vinegar and kosher salt and mix well. Chill, covered, for 1 hour or longer.

For the chicken, mix the olive oil, garlic, chili powder, oregano, cumin and kosher salt in a bowl.

Rub over the chicken. Marinate, covered, in the refrigerator for 30 minutes.

Grill the chicken over hot coals for 10 minutes or until cooked through. Serve with the salsa.

You may reserve any unused salsa in the refrigerator for another use.

Grilled Pizza

Pizza Crusts

3$^1/_2$ cups bread flour

1 package (2$^1/_4$ teaspoons)
dry yeast

1 tablespoon sugar

1 tablespoon salt

1$^1/_4$ cups (110- to 120-degree)
water

2 tablespoons extra-virgin
olive oil

Suggested Toppings

Central Market Tomato Basil
Marinara Sauce

sliced grilled chicken

grilled sliced onions

sliced kalamata olives

arugula

coarsely chopped green
bell peppers

sliced portobello mushrooms

cherry tomato halves

shredded mozzarella cheese

SERVES 5

For the crusts, combine the bread flour, yeast, sugar and salt in a bowl. Add the water and olive oil and mix to form a dough. Knead on a lightly floured surface or knead with a dough hook for 15 minutes or until the dough is smooth and elastic.

Place in an oiled bowl, turning to oil the surface. Let rise, covered, in a warm place for 1 hour or until doubled in bulk. Punch down the dough. Divide into 5 equal portions and cover with a towel. Let stand for 10 minutes.

Stretch or roll each portion into a round $^1/_8$ to $^1/_4$ inch thick. Place the rounds on a grill rack. Grill, covered, over medium coals for 2 to 3 minutes or until the bottoms begin to brown. Slide the crust rounds onto a baking sheet or a cool section of the grill and turn them over.

For the toppings, arrange your choices over the crusts. Return to the grill and grill, covered, for 5 minutes; do not overcook.

Romesco Sauce for Grilled Seasonal Vegetables

2 ancho chiles

1 tablespoon olive oil

1 (1/4-inch) slice
country-style bread

4 garlic cloves, chopped

1/3 cup hazelnuts, toasted
and peeled

1/2 cup blanched
almonds, toasted

2 roasted red bell peppers

2 tablespoons tomato paste

1/4 cup red wine vinegar,
or to taste

4 teaspoons smoked
Spanish paprika

1/2 teaspoon cayenne pepper,
or to taste

3/4 cup olive oil

salt to taste

SERVES 6 TO 8

Combine the ancho chiles with enough water to cover in a saucepan. Bring to a boil and remove from the heat. Let stand for 20 minutes; drain. Cut into pieces, discarding the stems and seeds.

Heat 1 tablespoon olive oil in a small skillet over medium heat. Add the bread and sauté for 3 to 5 minutes or until both sides are crisp and golden brown, turning once. Tear the bread into pieces and combine with the garlic, hazelnuts and almonds in a food processor. Process to the consistency of coarse meal. Add the ancho chiles, bell peppers, tomato paste, vinegar, paprika and cayenne pepper. Process until well mixed, scraping down the side of the container several times.

Add 3/4 cup olive oil in a fine stream, processing constantly until smooth. Season with salt and adjust the vinegar and cayenne pepper if desired.

Served over grilled seasonal vegetables, such as onions, asparagus, squash and tomatoes.

You may prepare the sauce in advance and store in a covered container in the refrigerator. Allow to return to room temperature before serving.

Hatch, New Mexico, is the self-proclaimed "Chile Capital of the World." The little town just outside Las Cruces usually has a population of about 1,000, but during the Hatch Chile Festival, Hatch's population swells to about 14,000—all of them certified hot-heads who will eat chiles on anything, from eggs to ice cream.

Central Market also honors the chile harvest with a festival. We don't draw quite the crowd that Hatch does, but hundreds of people crowd the stores in August and September when the crop comes in. "I was born in New Mexico and was practically raised on chiles," one customer told us, "but every year I come to Central Market in Austin for the Hatch event. It's hard to explain, but when I get a whiff of that smoky air and see those big roasters outside the store, it feels like a much bigger deal than it ever did at home. And when you go inside and have a taste of the Hatch pesto and the Hatch chile burger, I think that maybe these chiles were born in New Mexico, but they grew up in Austin."

Pot Roast with Green Chile Gravy

3 tablespoons olive oil

1 (6-pound) whole eye of round, trimmed

2 cups thinly sliced onions

2 garlic cloves, minced or pressed

1 (14^1/2-ounce) can diced tomatoes

8 cups beef stock or beef broth

2 tablespoons Worcestershire sauce

2 bay leaves

2 tablespoons chili powder

^{1}/2 teaspoon crumbled oregano leaves

1 teaspoon salt

2 cups chopped roasted green chiles, skins and seeds removed

1 cup water

^{1}/2 cup flour

salt and pepper to taste

SERVES 6

Heat the olive oil in a large heavy saucepan over high heat until it shimmers. Add the beef and brown on all sides. Remove the roast to a platter. Add the onions to the saucepan and sauté for 10 minutes or until tender. Add the garlic and sauté for 2 minutes longer.

Purée the undrained tomatoes in a blender. Add the tomatoes, beef stock, Worcestershire sauce, bay leaves, chili powder, oregano and 1 teaspoon salt to the saucepan and bring to a boil. Add the beef and green chiles. Simmer, tightly covered, over low heat for 3 to 3^1/2 hours or until the beef is fork-tender, turning occasionally. Remove the roast to an ovenproof platter and keep warm in a 250-degree oven.

Whisk the water gradually into the flour in a bowl to make a thin smooth paste. Bring the cooking liquid in the saucepan to a boil and add the paste gradually, stirring constantly. Cook until thickened, stirring constantly. Reduce the heat and cook the gravy, uncovered, at a low boil for 20 minutes. Season with salt and pepper to taste and discard the bay leaves.

Cut the roast into ^{1}/2-inch slices with a sharp knife and arrange on the platter. Ladle some of the gravy over the slices and serve with the remaining gravy.

CM Hatch Chile Pesto

6 mild or hot Hatch chiles, or a combination to suit your taste

1/2 cup (2 ounces) shredded Parmigiano-Reggiano cheese

1/2 cup packed fresh cilantro leaves

2 large garlic cloves

1/4 cup pecan pieces

2 tablespoons (or more) fresh lime juice

1 teaspoon salt, or to taste

1/2 cup olive oil

MAKES 1 1/2 CUPS

Place the chiles directly on a high gas flame or under a broiler and cook until charred on all sides. Place in a bowl and cover tightly with plastic wrap. Let stand for 15 to 20 minutes or until cool. Slip the skins from the chiles and discard the stems and seeds, wearing rubber gloves.

Combine the chiles, Parmigiano-Reggiano cheese, cilantro, garlic, pecans, 2 tablespoons lime juice and salt in a food processor fitted with a steel blade. Process until chopped. Add the olive oil gradually, processing constantly until the mixture forms a smooth paste. Taste and season with additional lime juice and salt if necessary. Store, covered, in the refrigerator for up to 1 week. Serve as a sauce for pasta, pork, chicken or seafood, or use as a dressing for salad.

CM loves the distinctive spicy flavor and moderate heat of Hatch chiles when they are in season. When they are out of season, you can substitute Anaheim chiles for a mild flavor and poblano chiles for a spicier pesto. One poblano chile equals 1 1/2 Hatch chiles, so adjust the recipe accordingly.

Southwestern Strata

2 pounds chorizo

2 tablespoons olive oil

3 cups chopped onions

2 cups chopped roasted fresh or canned Hatch green chiles

6 cups crushed tortilla chips

5 cups (1 1/4 pounds) shredded sharp Cheddar cheese

6 eggs

1 tablespoon chili powder

1 tablespoon ground cumin

1 1/2 teaspoons seasoned salt

4 cups (1 quart) milk

SERVES 8 TO 10

Remove and discard the casing from the sausage. Cook the sausage in a nonstick skillet over medium-high heat, stirring until brown and crumbly. Remove the sausage with a slotted spoon to drain on paper towels. Drain the skillet and add the olive oil and onions. Sauté for 10 minutes or until the onions are tender and translucent. Remove the onions with a slotted spoon and combine with the sausage and green chiles in a bowl; mix well.

Spread 2 cups of the tortilla chips in a even layer in a 9×13-inch baking dish sprayed with nonstick cooking spray. Layer half the sausage mixture and 2 cups of the cheese in the prepared dish. Repeat the layers. Mix the remaining cup of cheese with the remaining 2 cups of tortilla chips in a bowl and sprinkle over the top; press down lightly to compact.

Beat the eggs in a bowl. Add the chili powder, cumin and seasoned salt; mix well. Add the milk and beat until smooth. Pour carefully over the layers. Cover with plastic wrap and chill in the refrigerator for 8 hours or longer.

Place the oven rack in the top third of an oven preheated to 350 degrees. Place the baking dish in a larger baking pan and add enough hot water to reach just halfway up the side of the baking dish. Bake for 60 to 70 minutes or until set and golden brown. Cool for 10 minutes and cut into squares to serve. Serve with warm salsa if desired.

There are literally thousands of different kinds of chile peppers, but Hatch chiles stand out—not for their heat, but for a unique, mellow flavor that's enhanced through careful roasting. There are several varieties of Hatch chiles, too.

One of our favorites is the Big Jim, a distinctively large, thick and meaty chile with medium heat. It's named for a Hatch chile farmer, the late Jim Rutherford, who assisted researchers at New Mexico State University in developing it. We like the idea of someone leaving a chile pepper as his legacy and thank Big Jim every harvest.

Hatch Green Chile Stew

2 pounds boneless pork, cut into cubes

2 tablespoons olive oil

1/2 cup chopped onion

1 garlic clove, minced

1/4 cup flour

2 1/2 cups chopped peeled fresh tomatoes

1 3/4 cups chopped peeled roasted Hatch green chiles

1/2 teaspoon sugar

1 teaspoon salt

1 teaspoon pepper

2 potatoes, coarsely chopped

2 1/2 to 3 cups chicken broth

SERVES 6 TO 8

Brown the pork lightly in the olive oil in a large saucepan over medium heat. Add the onion and garlic and sauté for 3 to 4 minutes or until the onion is tender. Stir in the flour. Cook for 1 to 2 minutes or until smooth, stirring constantly.

Stir in the tomatoes, green chiles, sugar, salt and pepper. Add the potatoes and chicken broth. Reduce the heat and simmer, covered, for 1 to 1 1/2 hours or until the pork is tender.

Green Chile Cornbread

1¹/2 cups yellow cornmeal

¹/2 cup flour

1¹/2 teaspoons baking powder

1 tablespoon sugar

1 teaspoon ground cumin

1 teaspoon salt

1¹/4 cups buttermilk

³/4 cup chopped peeled roasted Hatch green chiles

1 egg

6 tablespoons (³/4 cup) butter, melted

SERVES 6

Sift the cornmeal, flour, baking powder, sugar, cumin and salt together. Combine the buttermilk, green chiles, egg and butter in a large bowl and mix well. Add the dry ingredients all at once and mix just until smooth; do not overmix.

Spoon the batter into a generously greased 8×8-inch baking pan. Bake at 400 degrees on the center oven rack for 30 minutes or until the top is light brown and a wooden pick inserted into the center comes out clean. Remove to a wire rack and cool for 10 minutes. Cut into squares to serve.

You may substitute bacon drippings or melted lard for the butter in this recipe. Reduce the salt to ¹/2 teaspoon when using bacon drippings.

CM prescribes chiles as good medicine for headaches, the pain of arthritis and even cold feet. They will improve the ratio of HDL to LCL cholesterol, boost the metabolic rate and improve the memory.

Hatch Green Chile Apple Cobbler

Filling

5 or 6 Granny Smith or Gala apples, peeled and sliced

2/3 cup packed brown sugar

1/2 cup chopped peeled roasted Hatch chiles

1 teaspoon cider vinegar

1/4 teaspoon cinnamon

1/8 teaspoon allspice

1/8 teaspoon nutmeg

1/4 teaspoon salt

Cobbler Topping

1 1/4 cups flour

1 cup sugar

grated zest of 2 lemons

1/8 teaspoon cinnamon

1/8 teaspoon nutmeg

1/8 teaspoon salt

3/4 cup (1 1/2 sticks) butter

2 tablespoons heavy cream

SERVES 8 TO 10

For the filling, combine the apples, brown sugar, green chiles, vinegar, cinnamon, allspice, nutmeg and salt in a bowl and mix well. Spoon into greased baking ramekins.

For the topping, mix the flour, sugar, lemon zest, cinnamon, nutmeg and salt in a bowl. Cut in the butter until crumbly. Stir in the cream.

Spread the topping over the apple mixture and press firmly. Bake at 375 degrees for 45 to 50 minutes or until brown and bubbly.

You may prepare the cobbler in a greased 9×9-inch baking pan if preferred.

Mardi Gras was the theme of Central Market's grand opening event in San Antonio. CM's parent company, H-E-B, has headquarters in San Antonio and has been selling groceries in Texas for nearly 100 years, but when we started remodeling that H-E-B store into a Central Market, we confused some customers and feared losing them.

For the grand opening, two jazz bands played all day, and every hour, employees paraded through the store. There was King Cake, gumbo, bread pudding and lot of beads to throw around. Each part of the store was decorated to look like a Mardi Gras float. The produce department had a table of crudités with a "marble" bust of a Greek god for a centerpiece. It was actually a Partner painted white who stood there all day with his head through a hole in the table. Occasionally, he would holler at unsuspecting customers. (Well, people always expect to find the unexpected at Central Market, don't they?)

We had no idea how many people would show up, but we ended up with an overflow crowd. The community welcomed our new idea so warmly and so completely that Mardi Gras became a signature event at Central Markets.

CM Gumbo

2/3 cup vegetable oil

2/3 cup flour

1 teaspoon dried thyme
leaves, crumbled

1 teaspoon dried oregano
leaves, crumbled

1 bay leaf

2 teaspoons gumbo filé powder

1/4 teaspoon cayenne pepper

12 ounces andouille sausage,
cut lengthwise into halves and
sliced 1/4 inch thick

1 1/2 cups chopped onions

1 1/2 cups chopped green
bell peppers

1 1/2 cups chopped celery

1 tablespoon minced garlic

3 to 4 cups water

2 cups bottled clam juice

1 1/2 cups coarsely chopped
cooked chicken

1 1/2 cups peeled and deveined
uncooked shrimp

1/4 teaspoon Louisiana hot sauce

hot cooked rice

SERVES 6 TO 8

Heat the oil in a large heavy saucepan over medium-high heat. Stir in the flour and reduce the heat to medium. Cook for 12 minutes or until the mixture is dark brown, stirring constantly and taking care not to let the mixture burn.

Add the thyme, oregano, bay leaf, filé powder and cayenne pepper and cook for 1 minute, stirring constantly. Add the sausage, onions, bell peppers, celery and garlic. Cook for 5 minutes or until the vegetables are tender, stirring constantly. Whisk in the water and clam juice and bring to a boil. Reduce the heat and simmer for 20 minutes.

Stir in the chicken and shrimp. Cook for 5 minutes or just until the shrimp are tender. Add the hot sauce, adjust the seasonings as needed and discard the bay leaf. Ladle over hot rice in bowls and serve with additional hot sauce.

You may reserve the shells from the shrimp and simmer, covered, in a mixture of the clam juice and water for 20 minutes. Strain the mixture to use in the recipe for added flavor.

Crawfish Chowder

2 tablespoons cornstarch

2 cups fish stock, clam juice or water

2 cups chopped onions

2 cups chopped Yukon Gold or russet potatoes

1 cup chopped celery

2 large garlic cloves, minced

2 cups half-and-half

1 teaspoon dried basil

1 teaspoon dried thyme

12 ounces crawfish meat

1/4 teaspoon cayenne pepper

salt and black pepper to taste

4 teaspoons unsalted butter, softened

4 teaspoons chopped parsley

SERVES 4

Dissolve the cornstarch in a small amount of the fish stock. Combine the remaining fish stock with the onions, potatoes, celery, garlic, half-and-half, basil and thyme in a large heavy saucepan. Bring to a boil over medium heat. Reduce the heat and simmer for 10 to 15 minutes or until the vegetables are tender. Remove from the heat.

Stir the cornstarch mixture into the hot chowder. Return the saucepan to low heat and add the crawfish and cayenne pepper. Cook for several minutes or just until the crawfish are cooked through, stirring constantly. Season with salt and black pepper to taste.

Ladle the chowder into large soup bowls. Top each serving with 1 teaspoon of butter and sprinkle with the parsley. Serve immediately.

You may serve the chowder in a hollowed-out small round sourdough or pain au levain loaf fitted with a small bowl or lined with cabbage leaves. You may also substitute crabmeat or small shrimp for the crawfish.

Herb-Stuffed Standing Rib Roast

1 (5- to 7-pound) standing rib roast (3 ribs)

3 large garlic cloves, sliced

1/2 bunch fresh sage, stems trimmed and minced

1/4 bunch fresh oregano, stems trimmed and minced

1/2 bunch fresh rosemary, stems trimmed and minced

1/2 bunch fresh tarragon, stems trimmed and minced

kosher salt and freshly ground pepper to taste

2 cups prepared demi-glace

SERVES 6

Cut the meat from the bones with a sharp knife, starting at the narrow end of the roast and leaving the ribs attached by about 1 inch at the meaty end to form a pocket. Place the garlic, sage, oregano, rosemary and tarragon evenly in the pocket and tie the meat to the bones with kitchen twine. Let stand at room temperature for 45 to 60 minutes.

Place the oven rack in the lower third of an oven preheated to 400 degrees. Place the roast on a rack in a roasting pan. Sprinkle generously with kosher salt and pepper. Insert a meat thermometer into the thickest portion, not touching the bone. Roast for 25 minutes.

Pour 1/4 inch water into the roasting pan and reduce the oven temperature to 375 degees. Roast for 50 minutes. Reduce the oven temperature to 350 degrees and roast for 20 minutes per pound. Add water to the roasting pan as needed to create steam, which helps the herbs to flavor the meat and protects the pan from the heat.

Roast to 125 degrees on the meat thermometer for medium-rare, to 135 degrees for medium and to 150 degrees for well done.

Remove from the oven and let stand for 15 to 20 minutes. Skim the pan juices and mix with the demi-glace in a bowl. Carve the roast and serve with the demi-glace mixture.

Cream of Pumpkin Soup with Sherry

$^1/_4$ cup ($^1/_2$ stick) butter

2 garlic cloves, minced

3 medium apples, peeled and chopped

2 pounds pie pumpkin, peeled and chopped

6 cups chicken broth

1 cup dry sherry

2 cups heavy cream

$^1/_2$ teaspoon cinnamon

$^1/_2$ teaspoon nutmeg

$^1/_4$ teaspoon cardamom

honey to taste

salt and freshly ground pepper to taste

SERVES 6

Melt the butter in a saucepan over medium-high heat. Add the garlic and sauté until fragrant. Add the apples, pumpkin and chicken broth. Bring to a boil and reduce the heat. Simmer for 15 minutes or until the pumpkin is tender, stirring occasionally. Stir in the sherry. Return to a boil and cook for 10 minutes longer.

Process the soup in batches in a blender until smooth. Combine the batches in the saucepan. Stir in the cream, cinnamon, nutmeg and cardamom. Simmer to the desired consistency. Season with honey, salt and pepper.

You may substitute butternut squash, delicata squash or any firm winter squash for the pumpkin in this recipe.

Holiday Chicken Salad

4 bone-in chicken breasts, poached with herbs
and aromatic vegetables

1/2 cup dried cranberries

3 to 4 tablespoons cranberry horseradish sauce

1/2 cup slivered almonds

1/2 cup chopped celery

salt and freshly ground pepper to taste

3/4 to 1 cup mayonnaise

SERVES 6

Debone the chicken, discarding the skin and bones. Cut into bite-size pieces. Combine with the cranberries, cranberry horseradish sauce, almonds, celery, salt and pepper in a bowl. Add the mayonnaise and mix well. Chill until serving time.

You may substitute 3 tablespoons whole cranberry sauce and 1 tablespoon prepared horseradish for the cranberry horseradish sauce if preferred.

CM has a line of themed holiday baskets that make perfect gifts. They range from simple to elaborate and reflect the variety of top-quality products available at Central Market. We can also assist you in customizing a basket to suit the personal style of the recipient.

Acorn Squash with
Cranberry and Mushroom Stuffing

2 small acorn squash

olive oil

1 cup dried cranberries

1/4 cup minced shallots

1 teaspoon minced garlic

2 tablespoons unsalted butter

3/4 cup chopped button or
cremini mushrooms

1/4 cup chopped shiitake
mushroom caps

1 tablespoon grated orange zest

1/2 teaspoon dried
Mexican oregano

2 cups fresh bread crumbs

vegetable stock

1/2 teaspoon salt

1/4 teaspoon pepper

2 tablespoons unsalted butter

SERVES 4

Cut the squash into halves lengthwise and discard the seeds. Brush the cut sides lightly with olive oil. Place cut side down on a baking sheet. Bake at 425 degrees for 20 minutes or just until tender.

Combine the dried cranberries with enough water to cover in a microwave-safe bowl. Microwave on High for 4 minutes. Let stand until cool and drain.

Sauté the shallots and garlic in 2 tablespoons melted butter in a heavy skillet over medium heat for 3 to 4 minutes or until tender. Add the mushrooms, orange zest and oregano. Sauté for 3 to 4 minutes or until the mushrooms are tender. Add the bread crumbs and sauté until light brown, stirring constantly. Stir in the cranberries and enough vegetable stock to moisten. Season with the salt and pepper.

Spoon the mushroom mixture into the cavities of the squash and arrange the squash on the baking sheet. Dot with 2 tablespoons butter. Bake for 10 to 15 minutes or until heated through and golden brown.

Frying Pan Holiday Cookies

1/2 cup (1 stick) butter

1 cup sugar

1/2 teaspoon salt

2 eggs, beaten

1 cup chopped dates

1 cup walnut pieces

1 (4-ounce) jar maraschino cherries, drained and cut into halves

1 teaspoon vanilla extract

2 cups crisp rice cereal

1 1/2 cups flaked coconut

MAKES 2 TO 3 DOZEN

Melt the butter in a frying pan. Stir in the sugar and salt and cook until the sugar dissolves. Remove from the heat and let stand until cool. Add the eggs, dates, walnuts, cherries and vanilla and mix well. Cook for 5 to 6 minutes or until thickened, stirring constantly.

Remove from the heat and stir in the cereal. Shape into walnut-size balls and roll in the coconut, coating evenly. Place on waxed paper and let stand until firm. Store in an airtight container.

Doc was all set to "cook his way across the country" after he graduated from culinary school in California. He had gotten as far as Texas when Central Market first opened, and he served chocolate crêpes to Texas Governor Ann Richards at the store's opening gala.

Before long, "Doc" was a regular, taking care of the produce and talking to customers about food. "I love this place because it's always different," he says. "You see the seasons change right on the shelves." Now Doc stays put, and the country comes to him.

COOKING SCHOOL

To be honest, we weren't really sure our Cooking School

would work. Our first instructors were our own Central Market

Partners, but it wasn't long before we started inviting

chefs from all over. A turning point came in 1997, when we invited

all ten of Food & Wine magazine's Best New Chefs

in the United States—and all ten accepted.

Today, we teach more students each year than any other

cooking school in the country. It's impossible to measure the

impact the schools have had, sparking interest in new cuisines,

forging lasting friendships and connections,

even inspiring dramatic career moves.

Years ago, Deborah Madison founded Greens, the famous vegetarian restaurant in San Francisco. But these days, her books and articles are focused on home cooking because, "It's important to know how to feed ourselves, to not turn it over to strangers," she says. "When you know where your food comes from—a traceable meal—you are suddenly connected to where you live in a much more profound way."

Obviously, Deborah and Central Market make a good match—we both believe in paying close attention to our food. Where is your food from? Who grew it and how? How did it get to you? "It's the opposite of fast food," says Deborah. That doesn't mean cooking has to take a long time, as her students have learned. It just means we should take time to enjoy what we eat. Easy to do when Deborah's cooking.

Three-Beet Caviar Salad with Endive and Goat Cheese

by Chef Deborah Madison

3/4 cup finely chopped red onion

3 tablespoons white wine vinegar or rice vinegar

sugar to taste

1/4 teaspoon salt

2 red beets

2 golden beets

2 chiogga beets

salt and pepper to taste

1 red and 1 white endive

olive oil

4 ounces (1 cup) crumbled fresh goat cheese

2 tablespoons chopped parlsey or fresh marjoram

freshly ground pepper to taste

SERVES 4

Combine the onion with the vinegar, sugar and 1/4 teaspoon salt in a bowl. Let stand for 30 minutes.

Cut off the stems of the beets, leaving 1 inch of the stems, the roots and skins. Steam the beets in separate saucepans for 25 to 45 or until tender-firm when pierced. Cool to room temperature and slip off the skins with oiled hands to prevent staining.

Shred the beets separately and place in separate bowls. Add 1/3 of the onion mixture to each bowl. Season with salt and pepper to taste and toss to mix well. Chill in the refrigerator.

Arrange mounds of each of the beets on individual salad plates. Separate the endives into leaves. Alternate leaves of the red and white endives on the plate. Drizzle with olive oil and sprinkle with the goat cheese, parsley and freshly ground pepper.

Wild Mushroom Salad
with Corn and Mustard Dressing

by Chef John Ash

Corn Mustard Dressing

2 tablespoons minced shallots

2 teaspoons minced poached or roasted garlic

1/4 cup double-strength unsalted chicken broth or vegetable broth

1 tablespoon Dijon mustard

1/2 cup Spectrum Naturals unrefined corn oil

1 teaspoon fresh lemon juice

sea salt and freshly ground pepper to taste

Honey Lemon Vinaigrette

2 tablespoons minced shallot

6 tablespoons seasoned rice vinegar

2 tablespoons fragrant honey

1/4 cup fresh lemon juice

1/4 cup olive oil

Salad

3 tablespoons clarified butter or olive oil

11/2 pounds wild mushrooms, such as shiitake, chanterelle or oyster

sea salt and freshly ground pepper to taste

8 cups loosely packed young greens

fresh dill sprigs, fried capers and shaved Parmesan or dry Jack cheese

SERVES 6

For the dressing, combine the shallots, garlic and chicken broth in a blender and process until smooth. Add the Dijon mustard. Add the corn oil gradually, processing constantly until smooth. Stir in the lemon juice, sea salt and pepper. Store, covered, in the refrigerator for up to 3 days.

For the vinaigrette, combine the shallot, vinegar, honey, lemon juice and olive oil in a bowl and whisk until well combined. Store, covered, in the refrigerator for up to 5 days.

For the salad, heat the clarified butter in a sauté pan and add the mushrooms. Sauté just until the mushrooms are tender but still hold their shape. Season with sea salt and pepper and keep warm. Toss the greens with just enough vinaigrette to moisten. Arrange the greens and mushrooms on a serving plate. Spoon the dressing around the salad and garnish with dill sprigs, fried capers and shaved Parmesan or dry Jack cheese. Serve immediately.

You could say **John Ash** is a missionary for California wine country cuisine—and, of course, at Central Market, we are as passionate as he is about the principles of seasonal cuisine and sustainable agriculture. John spreads the word through his award-winning cookbooks, television and radio shows and cooking classes. We do it on our shelves.

John came of cooking age in Northern California, where his Sonoma restaurant, John Ash and Company, won attention from Food & Wine magazine, which named him "Hot New Chef" in 1985. Since then, John has been culinary director for Fetzer Vineyards, a pioneer in organic wine and gardening.

He has taught at Central Market many times, and his classes are popular as much for his personal teaching style as for his recipes, which are undeniably elegant but easily achievable for the home cook.

*Television made **Martin Yan** a star, but years of hard work made him a great chef. Martin's father owned a restaurant in China, and his mother later ran a small grocery store. When he moved to Hong Kong at age 13, an uncle put him to work in his restaurant. Martin likes to joke that his first impression of Hong Kong was that it looked like the inside of a wok. He never dreamed that he would have a television show that would be shown worldwide, but his "Yan Can Cook," which first aired in 1978, is seen in more than 70 countries.*

Hong Kong Soft Beef Tacos

by Chef Martin Yan

2 tablespoons dark soy sauce

1 teaspoon minced garlic

2 tablespoons cornstarch

12 ounces beef flank steak, thinly sliced across the grain

3 tablespoons vegetable oil

1/2 cup julienned carrot

8 ounces white button mushrooms, julienned

4 ounces fresh shiitake mushroom caps, julienned

4 ounces fresh wood ear mushrooms, julienned (optional)

5 Chinese chives or green onions, cut into 2-inch pieces

1/4 cup chicken stock

2 teaspoons cornstarch

1 tablespoon water

1/3 cup hoisin sauce

2 tablespoons chile sauce

6 (8-inch) flour tortillas

SERVES 4 TO 6

Mix the soy sauce, garlic and 2 tablespoons cornstarch in a bowl. Stir in the beef. Marinate for 10 minutes. Heat a wok over high heat and add 2 tablespoons of the oil, swirling the wok to coat evenly. Add the beef and stir-fry for 1 1/2 minutes or until no longer pink. Remove the beef from the wok.

Add the remaining 1 tablespoon of the oil to the wok and swirl to coat. Add the carrot, mushrooms and chives. Stir-fry for 2 1/2 minutes. Add the chicken stock and bring to a boil. Simmer for 1 minute. Return the beef to the wok. Dissolve 2 teaspoons cornstarch in the water in a small bowl. Stir into the beef in the wok. Cook until thickened, stirring constantly. Spoon the beef into a bowl.

Mix the hoisin sauce and chile sauce in a bowl. Spread about 2 teaspoons of the sauce mixture on each warm tortilla and top with 1/4 cup beef mixture. Fold the tortillas in half to serve.

172

Spicy Thai Pork

by Chef Don Skipworth

2 tablespoons vegetable oil

4 garlic cloves, minced

1 small onion, finely chopped

1 tablespoon red curry paste

8 ounces coarsely ground lean pork

1 tablespoon sugar

2 to 3 tablespoons fish sauce

2 to 3 tablespoons lime juice

1 or 2 medium tomatoes, chopped

3 or 4 scallions, thinly sliced

1/2 (6-ounce) can tomato paste, or to taste

chile flakes to taste

1 or 2 medium tomatoes, chopped

cucumber sticks, cabbage leaves, lettuce leaves, Thai eggplant sticks and/or pork rind for dipping

SERVES 4 TO 6

Heat a skillet or wok over medium heat and add the oil. Add the garlic, onion and curry paste. Cook until the mixture is roasted and fully aromatic, taking care not to burn. Add the ground pork and cook until no longer pink.

Add the sugar, fish sauce, lime juice, 1 or 2 tomatoes and the scallions; mix well. Add just enough tomato paste to produce a smooth thick sauce. Cook until the desired consistency. Add chile flakes and adjust the seasonings.

Spoon into a serving bowl and top with 1 or 2 chopped tomatoes. Place in the center of a platter and serve with the vegetables and pork rind for dipping. You may also serve with tortilla chips and refried beans.

His name is **Don Skipworth,** but everybody calls him "Skip"— even his good friend Julia Child, who lives near him in Santa Barbara, California. Skip visits her just about every week. They dine together and go to movies and talk food—Skip's favorite topic.

Skip is a paradox of sorts. He grew up in the Texas Panhandle but learned to cook in the kitchen of a Chinese family with whom he was very close. His passion for Asian cooking became intense, and he eventually visited China and studied all of its regional cooking styles. These days, Skip finds adventure in exploring the fusion of Eastern and Western foods.

Chicken in Pueblan Green Pumpkin Seed Sauce

by Chef Rick Bayless

Chicken

1 (3-pound) chicken

8 cups (2 quarts) water

1/2 cup sliced white onion

2 garlic cloves, coarsely chopped

1/2 cup thinly sliced carrot

1 teaspoon salt

2 bay leaves

1/4 teaspoon dried thyme

1/4 teaspoon dried marjoram

Pueblan Green Pumpkin Seed Sauce

1 cup (about 4 1/2 ounces) hulled pumpkin seeds

1/2 cup sliced white onion

12 large cilantro sprigs, coarsely chopped

3 small romaine leaves, coarsely chopped

2 large radish leaves, coarsely chopped

3 serrano chiles, coarsely chopped, or 2 small jalapeño chiles, coarsely chopped

2 garlic cloves, coarsely chopped

1 tablespoon vegetable oil or olive oil

reserved chicken broth

1/2 teaspoon salt

SERVES 4

For the chicken, separate the neck, heart, giblets and back. Cut the remaining chicken into quarters. Bring the water to a boil in a 6-quart saucepan. Add the onion, garlic, carrot, salt, chicken back, neck, heart and giblets. Cook until foam rises to the surface and skim off the foam. Simmer, partially covered, over medium-low heat for 20 minutes.

Add the dark meat quarters and return to a simmer. Skim the foam again and add the bay leaves, thyme and marjoram. Cook, partially covered, over medium heat for 10 minutes. Add the white meat quarters and return to a simmer. Skim the foam and cook, partially covered, for 13 minutes. Cool the chicken in the broth for several minutes. Remove the chicken from the broth, reserving the broth for the sauce.

Strain the chicken broth, spooning off any fat as it cools. Reserve for the sauce.

For the sauce, sprinkle the pumpkin seeds in a heavy 10- to 12-inch skillet. Toast over medium heat until the seeds begin to pop from flat to rounded and turn golden brown, stirring frequently. Toast for 5 minutes or until all the seeds have popped. Spread on a plate to cool.

Reserve 2 tablespoons of the pumpkin seeds. Combine the remaining pumpkin seeds with the onion, cilantro sprigs, romaine leaves, radish leaves, chiles and garlic in a blender. Add $1^1/2$ cups of the reserved broth. Process to a smooth purée.

Heat the oil in a heavy 4-quart saucepan over medium heat. Add the purée and cook for 10 minutes or until very thick, stirring constantly. Stir in 2 cups of the reserved broth. Simmer, partially covered, for 20 minutes.

Spoon into a blender and process to a smooth purée, adding additional broth or water if necessary for a medium consistency. Rinse the saucepan and return the sauce to the pan.

Add the salt and chicken. Heat just below a simmer over medium-low heat for 10 minutes.

Remove the chicken to a warm serving platter with a slotted spoon. Ladle the sauce over the top. Garnish with the reserved pumpkin seeds and additional cilantro sprigs.

A *literal journey put **Rick Bayless** on the path to culinary fame. His family owned a string of barbecue restaurants in Oklahoma City, so he knew how to cook. He got the bug to expand his culinary horizons while studying Spanish and Latin American culture in college. Later, he traveled throughout Mexico for six years to learn the distinct regional styles.*

Rick serves up amazing Mexican food at his two restaurants, Frontera Grill and Topolobombo. With his cookbooks and television shows, he somehow manages to strike the perfect balance between authoritative and just plain friendly. When he taught at one of the Central Market schools in 2002, students were spellbound as he showed them how to make guacamole and properly roast tomatillos for a salsa. It's not that the techniques were foreign to them: it's that Rick's enthusiasm for the cultures and traditions surrounding Mexican cooking is remarkable—and contagious.

Smoked Trout Hash with
Spicy Ketchup and Sunny-Side Eggs

by Chef Terry Conlan

3/4 cup ketchup

1 teaspoon Tabasco sauce

1 1/2 tablespoons light corn syrup

1 tablespoon cider vinegar

8 cups (1/4-inch) cubes peeled Idaho potatoes

3 tablespoons olive oil

1 1/2 cups chopped onions

4 garlic cloves, minced

2 teaspoons minced fresh rosemary

salt and pepper to taste

12 ounces smoked rainbow trout, flaked

2 tablespoons minced parsley

8 organic eggs

SERVES 8

Combine the ketchup, Tabasco sauce, corn syrup and vinegar in a bowl and mix well. Parboil the potatoes in boiling water in a saucepan for 2 minutes; drain and pat dry. Sauté the potatoes in the olive oil in a large nonstick skillet until crisp. Add the onions and sauté for 1 minute. Stir in the garlic, rosemary, salt and pepper. Add the trout and parsley and cook until heated through. Remove from the heat and keep warm.

Cook the eggs sunny-side up in a large nonstick skillet coated with nonstick cooking spray.

Drizzle some of the ketchup mixture in a zig-zag pattern onto 8 serving plates. Spoon the hash onto the prepared plates and top each with an egg. Drizzle the remaining ketchup mixture over the eggs and serve immediately.

It sounds like a cliché, or an exaggeration, but you really wouldn't know that *Terry Conlan's* food was low in fat unless he told you. Terry, executive chef at Lake Austin Spa Resort, is a master at cutting calories but not flavor. He does it by using very small amounts of strong ingredients like bacon or pancetta and enhancing their flavors to the maximum. He also insists on using the very best ingredients he can find. We could take a lesson from Terry, and, in fact, many of us do: Terry has taught more cooking classes at Central Market than any other guest chef.

Terry worked in the restaurant business for nearly 20 years before finding his niche in spa cuisine. And his creative work has not gone unnoticed. Lake Austin Spa Resort is considered to be one of the top spas in the nation.

Green Lightning Shrimp

by Chef Steven Raichlen

3/4 cup coarsely chopped stemmed cilantro

4 to 8 jalapeño chiles, seeded and coarsely chopped

1 bunch scallions, white and green portions,
trimmed and coarsely chopped

3 garlic cloves, coarsely chopped

1 teaspoon ground cumin

1 1/2 teaspoons kosher salt or sea salt

1 teaspoon freshly ground pepper

1/2 cup extra-virgin olive oil

1/2 cup fresh lime juice

2 1/2 pounds jumbo shrimp, peeled and deveined

Garlic Cilantro Butter (page 179)

SERVES 6

To marinate the shrimp, combine the cilantro, chiles, scallions, garlic, cumin, kosher salt and pepper in a food processor and process until finely chopped. Add the olive oil and lime juice gradually, processing constantly to a bright green purée.

Thread the shrimp onto twelve 10- to 12-inch metal or soaked bamboo skewers, using 2 parallel skewers for each kabob. Place in a shallow nonmetal dish and pour the marinade over the shrimp. Marinate in the refrigerator for 30 minutes, turning the kabobs several times.

To grill the shrimp, drain and discard the marinade. Place the kabobs on a heated grill brushed with oil. Grill for 1 to 3 minutes on each side or just until heated through and firm to the touch, basting with the Garlic Cilantro Butter.

Remove the shrimp to a platter and drizzle with any remaining butter. Serve with lime wedges.

Garlic Cilantro Butter

8 tablespoons (1 stick) butter

2 garlic cloves, minced

3 tablespoons coarsely chopped
stemmed cilantro

SERVES 6

Melt the butter in a saucepan over medium heat. Add the garlic and cilantro and sauté for 2 minutes or until the garlic is fragrant. Keep warm.

Becoming one of the world's top authorities on grilling wasn't easy work for Steven Raichlen. He traveled around the world to 25 countries in four years to research The Barbecue Bible. The book has sold more than two million copies and has established Steven as the go-to guy for questions about any aspect of cooking over coals.

Grilling is practically the official pastime in Texas, so that makes Steven a huge draw when he teaches at Central Market. When he's not on the road teaching, doing more research or signing books, he works as an instructor at Barbecue University at the esteemed Greenbrier Resort in West Virginia.

And yet, grilling isn't Steven's only passion. When asked what he'd order up for his last meal, Steven was quick with an answer that reveals his Mid-Atlantic roots: Maryland crabs steamed in beer, vinegar, rock salt and spices.

Praline Sweet Potato Casserole

by Chef Diane Morgan

Sweet Potatoes

6 large dark-orange-flesh sweet potatoes, scrubbed, about 5 1/2 pounds

1/2 cup (1 stick) unsalted butter

3/4 cup milk

3 eggs, lightly beaten

3/4 cup packed dark brown sugar

Praline Topping

1/4 cup (1/2 stick) unsalted butter

3/4 cup packed dark brown sugar

3/4 cup heavy cream

1 1/2 cups coarsely chopped pecans

1/2 teaspoon cinnamon

1/2 teaspoon freshly grated nutmeg

1/2 teaspoon salt

2 teaspoons vanilla extract

SERVES 8 TO 10

For the sweet potatoes, pierce each potato several times with a fork and arrange in a baking pan. Bake at 350 degrees for 1 1/4 to 1 1/2 hours or until the potatoes test tender when pierced with a fork. Let stand until cool enough to handle. Increase the oven temperature to 375 degrees.

Melt the butter with the milk in a small saucepan and heat until hot but not boiling. Cut the potatoes into halves and scoop into a large bowl, discarding the skins. Mash the potatoes with a potato masher, ricer or food mill. Stir in the milk mixture and whisk in the eggs. Add the brown sugar and mix until smooth. Spread evenly in a buttered 9×13-inch or round 11-inch baking dish.

For the topping, melt the butter in a 2-quart saucepan over low heat. Stir in the brown sugar, cream, pecans, cinnamon, nutmeg and salt. Bring to a simmer and cook for 5 minutes or until the brown sugar dissolves and the mixture is thickened.

Remove from the heat and stir in the vanilla. Spread evenly over the sweet potatoes.

Bake for 30 minutes or until the topping is set and slightly crusty. Serve immediately.

Knowing that food is at the heart of our dearest celebrations, **Diane Morgan** teaches students about all the details of a festive meal. She wants all of us to have a good time in the kitchen and at the table. Her classes at Central Market have the same emphasis on entertaining as her award-winning cookbooks, articles and television and radio appearances. Students learn how to serve up a feast, from shopping for and presenting the food to decorating the table. Diane even offers tips on what to do with leftovers—if there are any.

Artisanal has become the new buzzword in food, especially when referring to bread and cheese. But it's not news to Paula Lambert. More than 20 years ago, after failing to find the kind of cheese she had come to love in Italy, Paula decided to go to Italy to learn how to make cheeses herself. She peddled them out of her little downtown Dallas cheese factory, in the process befriending prestigious chefs across the country. Paula played an important part in the beginning of Southwest cuisine and was chosen for the James Beard Foundation's Who's Who of Food and Beverage in America in 1985.

Ricotta and Goat Cheese Crespelle

by Chef Paula Lambert

2 eggs

1 1/2 pounds drained ricotta cheese

1/4 cup (1 ounce) grated Parmigiano-Reggiano cheese

8 ounces fresh goat cheese

1 tablespoon minced fresh herbs

salt and ground pepper to taste

16 (6- to 8-inch) crêpes

1/4 cup (1 ounce) grated Parmigiano-Reggiano cheese

1 1/2 tablespoons butter, melted

3 cups tomato sauce, heated

6 fresh basil leaves, julienned

SERVES 6

Combine the eggs, ricotta cheese, 1/4 cup Parmigiano-Reggiano cheese, goat cheese and fresh herbs in a food processor; pulse just until mixed. Season with salt and pepper and chill.

Place 1 crêpe at a time on a work surface. Mound 3 to 4 tablespoons of the cheese filling evenly across the center of the crêpe from side edge to side edge. Roll the crêpe to enclose the filling. Repeat with the remaining crêpes and filling. Cut the crêpes crosswise into thirds with a sharp knife.

Stand the crêpe pieces on end with sides touching in a generously buttered 7×11-inch or 10×10-inch baking dish with low sides. Sprinkle with 1/4 cup Parmigiano-Reggiano cheese and drizzle with the melted butter.

Bake at 375 degrees for 30 to 45 minutes or until the edges are brown. Remove with a spatula and place 8 on each serving plate. Spoon the tomato sauce over several of the crespelle and in a pool to the side. Sprinkle with the basil.

Key Limes Filled with Shredded Coconut Cream

by Chef Susana Trilling

16 Key limes or clementines

2 quarts water

2 tablespoons baking soda

1 quart water

2 cups sugar

6 cups water

5 cups shredded fresh coconut

1/2 cup evaporated milk

1/2 cup coconut milk

1 cup sugar

2 cinnamon sticks

lime leaves and orange blossoms

SERVES 16

Trim the ends of the Key limes and cut into halves crosswise. Bring 2 quarts water and the baking soda to a boil in a saucepan. Add the limes and cook for 5 minutes; drain. Scoop the fruit from each rind shell, reserving the shells. Rinse in cold water. Bring 1 quart water to a boil in a saucepan. Add the lime shells and cook for 10 minutes; drain.

Bring 2 cups sugar and 6 cups water to a boil in a stainless steel saucepan. Add the lime shells and reduce the heat. Simmer for 50 to 60 minutes. Remove to a bowl with a slotted spoon and chill.

Combine the coconut, evaporated milk, coconut milk, 1 cup sugar and cinnamon sticks in a saucepan and mix well. Bring to a simmer and cook for just 10 minutes, stirring occasionally. Cool to room temperature and remove the cinnamon sticks. Spoon into the lime shells and arrange on a tray. Chill, covered with plastic, in the refrigerator.

Arrange a lime leaf and orange blossoms on each serving plate and add 2 lime halves to each plate. Sprinkle with additional orange blossom petals.

The regional cuisines of Mexico are as rich and distinct from one another as the cuisines of Italy. Susana Trilling's specialty is food from Oaxaca, the southern state of Mexico, where she has established her own cooking school and where she is still exploring, collecting new recipes and flavors from the local heritage. Like Central Market, she got her start in Austin. Like Central Market, she has expanded beyond the Austin city limits. Her readable cookbooks and popular PBS series invite you on a rich culinary tour of the seven regions of Oaxaca, an exotic and earthy experience she brings to her cooking classes at Central Market.

Caramel Apricot Nut Crumble Tart

by Chef Mary Cech

Tart Crust

1 cup (2 sticks) unsalted
butter, softened

1/2 cup sugar

1 egg

2 1/2 cups flour

1/2 teaspoon salt

Crumble Topping

1/2 cup (1 stick) unsalted
butter, softened

1/3 cup packed light brown sugar

1 cup (or more) flour

1/2 teaspoon salt

Filling

3/4 cup chopped dried apricots

1/3 cup unsalted butter

1/4 cup sugar

1 cup packed brown sugar

1/4 cup honey

3/4 cup finely chopped
macadamias

3/4 cup finely chopped walnuts

1/4 cup heavy cream

SERVES 8

For the crust, cream the butter and sugar in a mixing bowl until light and fluffy. Beat in the egg, scraping down the bowl. Add the flour and salt and mix to form a dough. Shape into a 6-inch ball and wrap in plastic wrap. Chill in the refrigerator.

Roll the chilled dough 1/8 inch thick on a lightly floured surface and fit into a fluted 9-inch tart pan with a removable side. Place the tart pan on a baking sheet with a rim and bake at 350 degrees for 25 minutes or until golden brown.

For the topping, combine the butter, brown sugar, flour and salt in a medium bowl and mix with the fingers until crumbly; the mixture should form clumps when squeezed. Add additional flour 1 tablespoon at a time if necessary for the correct consistency. Sprinkle over a parchment-lined baking sheet with a rim. Bake at 350 degrees on the center oven rack for 15 minutes, stirring once. Let stand until cool.

For the filling, sprinkle the apricots in the prepared crust. Combine the butter, sugar, brown sugar and honey in a saucepan. Bring to a boil, stirring to dissolve the sugar. Boil for 1 minute without stirring. Remove from the heat and add the macadamias, walnuts and cream. Pour over the apricots in the crust.

Bake at 350 degrees for 25 minutes or until the filling is bubbly and the nuts are brown. Sprinkle with the topping immediately. Cool to room temperature. Place on a serving plate and remove the side of the pan.

*For many people, dessert is the high point of the meal. So for many people, **Mary Cech's** classes at Central Market are a high point; we nearly always book every possible space. Twice recognized as one of the "Top Ten Pastry Chefs in America" by* Chocolatier *magazine, Cech has provided sweets for some of the finest kitchens in the country. She has created desserts for Charlie Trotter's, the Cypress Club, the Grand Wailea. She taught at the Culinary Institute of America's Greystone Campus in the Napa Valley and is now director of pastry arts for the Cook Street School of Fine Cooking in Denver, Colorado. So although she has had a lot of experience teaching professionals, Mary is a favorite at Central Market cooking classes because she also always has the home baker in mind.*

Acknowledgments

Special thanks to copy consultant Teresa Elliot and design consultant Larry Jarvis

Happy Abdelbaki
Jacqueline Abu-Amr
Jan Admire
Dee Allen
Turner Almond
D.S. Alvarez
Lisa Anderson
George Attal
Mary Ann Austin
Laura Ayres
Rosario Ballesteros
Diane A. Ballinger
Tania Bardyn
J. Marie Bassett
Douglas Bates
Sherry Beth Beard
Susanne Bednarzyk
Mary K. Beissner
Helen Benn
Bo Benn
Marvin Billings
Beverley A. Bishop
Shelley J. Bjorkman
Jan Blankenship
Thomas Blaschke
Mark Bober
Greg Braak
Don "Bubba" Breedlove
Geraldine Breen
Sarah Brightman
Susan Brisbin
Rhonda Brown
Mikey Brown
Sue Brown
Denise Brown
Adelle Brownlee Brewer
Lisa Gay Bryant

Will Burdette
William Caldwell
Melissa Calvillo
Terry Canady
Cindy Carl
Kari Carlton
Mauricio Carranza
Vickie Carter
Celeste Casey
Tammy Castanie
Carole Chaffee
Ginny Chadwick
Loanne Chiu
Lynne Parkhurst Ciuba
Peter R. Clarac
Garry Clifford
Ellen Clinton
Lark Coggins
Richard Cohen
Suzanna Cole
Alexis Collett
Elizabeth Corey
Lois Cortney
Kathi Cox
Sara Crismon
Jere Cudd & Corrine Steeger
Kay Dabney
Julie D'Amore
Cynthia Davis
Jane Davis
Tomas De La Mata
Ana Marie De Portela
Mary E. DeMuth
Florence Devany
Mary Jane Douglas
Sarah Dunnihoo
David Dyer

Ed Ebert
Carla Edlund
Jeannie Eisenberg
Lee Elsesser
Cindy Bighorse Escobedo
Lisa Estes
Beatrice M. Estrada
Carole Everhart
Barbara Fahrlender
Rita Falstad
Charlie M. Farr
Evie Feltoon
Anna Fletcher
Claudia Floyd
Roger B. Foltz
Barbara Forshey
Wanda D. Frederick
Doris Fuda
Bobbie Fuller
Derek Gabbard
Rhonda Gabbard
Linda Gartner
Dr. Anne Gervasi
Nancy Gore
Kathy Graig
Mitchell Granger
Mary Grelle
Shelley Grieshaber
Suzanne Gruber
Carolyn Hammons
Wendy Hancock
Ericka Hancock
Trent Hancock
Joel M. Harris
Jennifer Hartzke
Bill Hayes
Kathy Hehman

Ronda Hill
Joyce Hill
Sydney Mosher Hill
Bonnie Hobratsch
Vivian Holmes
Sarah Houle
Marilyn Howard
Candace Huff
Lou Ann Huffhines
Candy Jackson
Francisco Rocha Jaje
Valerie Jasinski
Jax
Melinda Jayson
Carolyn Johns
Anne Johnson
Mary L. Jones
Jane Keller
Katie Kelly
Ednamae Kinsman
Sue Kittrell
Christine Klimek
Jamie Knorr
Sharon Knowles
Linda Davis Kyle
P.A. Lagergren
Linda Lawson
Sally G. Lebourgeois
Peg Lee
Anne Legg
Claudia Patricia Leon
Fily Lerten
Miguel Linares
Lindsay Loughlin
Amy Love
Jamye Luevano
Kristin Lyon

Gloria Maltz
Gini & John Marston
Tina Martin
Nancy Martinez
Kim Martinez
Mary Martini
Laurie Mather
Pat Mc Cready
Michael McBeth
Dian McClain
Paula McCullough
Caroline McKee
Beverly McKendree
Vickie McKilliip
Lenore McLeland
Katherine Meredith
C. Gay Meyer
Vicki Midyett
Chance Miller
Leslie Miller
Jolene Miller
Roger Mollett
Janice Montiverdi
Christine Morris
Pam Murphy
Kayla Murray
Elie Nassar
Sharon Nelson
Sari Jane Newell
Sue Nicks
Ralph Niebuhr
Anna Norris
Belinda Norris
Jill Nowell
Faye Olney
Deborah Orrill
Louis Oritz

Bonnie A. Owen
Dean Owens
Connie Owens
Doris Paddison
Linda Parker
Jesse Parker
Cheryl Paul
Patricia Peoples
Jan Perry
Jay Petos
Mark Picker
Judy Pirtle
Kim Pottlizer
Ted Powers
Barbie Preston
Susan Pritchett
Janet Purvis
Tami Ramsay
Rosana Rangel
Anu Rao
Nicole Ray
Rosemary Rector
Joannie Reis
Sharon Richardson
Patrick J. Riordan
LeRoy Rivers
Darlene Roberts
Elizabeth Roberts
Ann Rochat
Karen Rose
Irene Rosen
Avis Rosenlund
David E. Ross
Jasmine Ross
Yvonne Rudolph
Erica Ryan
Rebecca Sacchetti

Patti Saitow
Jerry Salzberg
Carolyn C. Sanders
Kerri Schneider
Holly Schreiber
Mary Schroder
Heather Schwille
Peggy Scott
Cindee Segal
Mary Shy
Jesse Simmons
Terri Carpenter-Simon
Katie Simpson
Krista Sleeper
Linda Smith
Jennifer Smith
Linda Smith
Zoe Smith
Melissa Sneed
Martin & Sandra Southwick
Susan Spears
Craig Spitzberg
Swanee Splichal
Terri St. Arnauld
Pat Stady
Darlene Staffa
Mary Ann Steele
Beverly A. Stehle
Bill Stoner
Lilo Strait
Beatriz Tapia
Sherry Terry
Margaret Thibert
Janet Thibodeaux
Carolyn Thomas
Bonnie Malnati Thompson
Terri Thompson

Holli Ticknor
Lola Tinney
Doris M. Toubin
Kathy Trybula
Rebecca Turner
Marie Van Gilder
Jos van Wunnik
Lena Vasquez
Michael Venator
Eric Vogler
Barbara Wagner
Margaret Walsworth
Carole Waltrip
Laurel Waters
Karin Waymire
Virginia Wayne
Carolyn Wickwire
Brenda Lewis Williams
Christie Williams
Charles Winkler
Bob Wolfkill
Chris Wollenzier
Denice Woods
Jannifer V. Woodson
Georgann Wrinkle
Becky Wurmstein
Liz Wynne
Susan Zana
Bethany Zimbicki

INDEX

Sherry-Roasted Garlic Mashed
  Potatoes with Blue Cheese, 90
Southwestern Strata, 147
Spinach-Ricotta Filling, 84
Spring Mix with Toasted Pecans,
  Cranberries and Stilton in
  Sherry Vinaigrette, 25
Stilton Cheesecake, 114
Three-Beet Caviar Salad with
  Endive and Goat
  Cheese, 169
Tortellini with Smoked Turkey
  and Mozzarella, 62
Veal Chops Stuffed with Fontina
  and Prosciutto, 45
Wild Mushroom and Goat
  Cheese Quesadillas, 20

Cheesecakes
Curried Chutney Cheesecake, 16
Orange Dream
  Cheesecake, 115
Stilton Cheesecake, 114

Cherry
Cherry Port Reduction, 43
Dried Cherry and Hazelnut
  Bread Pudding, 113

Chicken
Asian Chicken Noodle
  Soup, 34
Chicken in Pueblan Green
  Pumpkin Seed Sauce, 174
Chicken Vegetable Soup with
  Cheese Tortellini, 33
CM Gumbo, 153
CM Tortilla Soup, 39
Grilled Chicken Breasts with
  Papaya, Cucumber and
  Tomato Salsa, 141
Holiday Chicken Salad, 163
Jambalaya, 155
Roast Chicken with Fresh
  Tarragon, 58
Seaport Paella, 74
Tandoori Chicken
  Sandwiches, 140

Chocolate
Chocolate Cakes with Melted
  Caramel Centers, 124
Chocolate Drizzle Icing, 123
Chocolate Mayonnaise Cake
  with Chocolate Drizzle
  Icing, 123
CM Cowboy Cookies, 131
Eiswein Truffles, 121
Mint-to-Be Ice Cream, 118
Outrageous Chocolate Chip
  Cookies, 129

Chutney
Chutney Topping, 16
Curried Chutney Cheesecake, 16
Texas Grapefruit Chutney, 61

Coconut
Best-Ever Cookies, 128
CM Coconut Macaroons, 130
Coconut and Lime Sauce, 69
Curried Chutney Cheesecake, 16
Frying Pan Holiday Cookies, 165
Key Limes Filled with Shredded
  Coconut Cream, 183

Cookies
Best-Ever Cookies, 128
CM Coconut Macaroons, 130
CM Cowboy Cookies, 131
Frying Pan Holiday Cookies, 165
Outrageous Chocolate Chip
  Cookies, 129

Cranberry
Acorn Squash with Cranberry
  and Mushroom Stuffing, 164
Holiday Chicken Salad, 163
Spring Mix with Toasted Pecans,
  Cranberries and Stilton in
  Sherry Vinaigrette, 25

Crusts
Almond Crust, 120
Cookie Crumb Crust, 115
Pizza Crusts, 142
Tart Crust, 184

Desserts. *See also* Cakes; Candy;
  Cheesecakes; Cookies;
  Puddings; Tarts
Basic Fresh Fruit Sorbet, 116
Coffee Granita with Sambuca
  Cream, 103
Hatch Green Chile Apple
  Cobbler, 151
Hazelnut Shortcakes with
  Fresh Berries and Ginger
  Cream, 111
Key Limes Filled with Shredded
  Coconut Cream, 183
Mint-to-Be Ice Cream, 118
Papaya Granita, 103
Tippie Creek Fruit Cobbler, 119
Watermelon Berry Granita, 103

Duck
Citrus-Glazed Roast Duck with
  Texas Grapefruit Chutney, 61
Country Cassoulet, 54

Egg Dishes
Eggnog French Toast with Maple
  Syrup, 99
Enchiladas de Huevos Verano, 76
Scrambled Eggs Supreme, 77
Smoked Trout Hash with Spicy
  Ketchup and Sunny-Side
  Eggs, 176
Southwestern Strata, 147

Eggplant
Caponata, 12
CM Eggplant Napoleon, 84

Fish. *See also* Salmon; Tuna
Blackened Red Snapper, 63
Sautéed Fish with Coconut and
  Lime Sauce, 69
Smoked Trout Hash with Spicy
  Ketchup and Sunny-Side
  Eggs, 176
Spicy Sautéed Fish with Olives
  and Tomatoes, 67
Texas Gulf Flounder with Herb
  Crust, 63